Learning That Never Ends

PRAISE FOR *LEARNING THAT NEVER ENDS*

"*Learning That Never Ends* gives us all pause to step back for a moment from data points and benchmarks and refocus our efforts on the true goal of education and that is to create a society where learning is not the attainment of a cut score but rather a way of life."

—**Alan N. Johnson**, deputy superintendent,
Woodland Hills SD, Pittsburgh, PA

"For all those students feeling the pressure to get 'A's' for college admission; for all those schools feeling the pressure of high stakes standardized math and reading tests; for all those parents who feel saddened to witness their young child's joy of learning wither as they grow older, come two voices of hope for a different future, where learning returns to its original form, as an exploration, as a personal journey of enlightenment that ever ends. This is not a book of mere advocacy. It is a profoundly practical guide for nurturing a child's spirit to learn for a lifetime, and by so doing ensuing all else will follow."

—**Joseph F. Merlino**, president, the twenty–first–century
partnership for STEM education, Conshohocken, PA

"In the era of accountability and standardized testing, Pearse and Dunwoody remain faithful to their mission to teach and learn by skillfully and successfully communicating their commitment to both the art and science of education. Teachers at every level will most assuredly profit from the decades of experience and success shared here by the authors."

—**Maryann C. Lanchoney**, MA, LDTC, interim department
chair for education, Cabrini College, Radnor, PA

Learning That Never Ends

Qualities of a Lifelong Learner

Margie Pearse and Mary Dunwoody

ROWMAN & LITTLEFIELD EDUCATION

A division of
ROWMAN & LITTLEFIELD
Lanham • New York • Toronto • Plymouth, UK

Published by Rowman & Littlefield Education
A division of Rowman & Littlefield
4501 Forbes Boulevard, Suite 200, Lanham, Maryland 20706
www.rowman.com

10 Thornbury Road, Plymouth PL6 7PP, United Kingdom

British Library Cataloguing in Publication Information Available

Library of Congress Cataloging-in-Publication Data Available

978-1-4758-0530-7 (cloth : alk. paper)—978-1-4758-0531-4 (pbk. : alk. paper)—ISBN 978-1-4758-0532-1 (electronic)

∞™ The paper used in this publication meets the minimum requirements of American National Standard for Information Sciences—Permanence of Paper for Printed Library Materials, ANSI/NISO Z39.48-1992.

Printed in the United States of America

Contents

Foreword

Having just completed year 38 in public education, I was intrigued when asked to pen this foreword.

As I read this book, it gave me an opportunity to reflect on my own love affair with learning. Yes, I was the classroom teacher who ardently looked forward to staff development days, who begged to attend workshops and conferences, who offered to burn up my personal days, and who gladly covered out-of-pocket expenses—all to bring back nuggets of information and new instructional strategies (often to my students' dismay).

I'm not sure how I came to be such an enthusiastic learner. I know I was "good at school," and as a classroom teacher I yearned to learn, so as to share it with my students. But truly, it didn't have to be just with my students—I was content to teach anyone I came across.

My pursuit of learning took me in a very circuitous route, resulting in earning my doctorate near the end of my career with having already accrued an inordinate amount of credits that had *not* led to degrees . . . just to learning. Nonetheless, my relentless pursuit of knowledge surely benefited me in my career as a teacher and administrator.

The term "lifelong learner" has been bandied about for a while now, but the thought of consciously teaching our students to thirst for knowledge is very appealing.

I've heard repeatedly that we are educating students for careers that do not yet exist, so it is our duty to teach our children *how* to learn.

In this book, written by my colleagues and lifelong learners (and sharers) Margie and Mary, you will find a plethora of activities and strategies to engage your students, feel successful, and learn how to learn. I love that they can be used and adapted K–12 (and I actually plan to use these with my graduate students, as well).

I have already used the information on conquering procrastination in chapter 1 to assist me in kickstarting this foreword.

I absolutely identified with the information regarding failure. At one point my administrative team worked closely with a former Army Ranger, who discussed how they learned more from missions that failed and used them as learning opportunities—failure paired with reflection leads to resilience.

The concept of "failure" is gaining some legs in education. Not only does it lead to creative insights (think the invention of Velcro), but it allows learners to develop grit—work that is currently being researched and shared by Seligman Research Associates at the University of Pennsylvania.

Read this book quickly, share the fabulous ideas with your colleagues, and then leave it by your lesson plans and consult it often.

Rina Vassallo, EdD

Preface

Stop for a minute before beginning this book. Go grab your district's mission statement, and bring it back. We bet somewhere in it is a challenge for you to empower your students to become lifelong learners.

Below you will find a range of mission statements from across the United States. They vary in many ways, but they all have one thing in common: the desire for students to become lifelong learners.

SOUTHEAST DELCO SCHOOL DISTRICT, COLLINGDALE, PENNSYLVANIA

The mission of the Southeast Delco School District is to nurture, educate, and challenge students to become *lifelong learners*, possessing knowledge, compassion, and a desire to serve the global community.

ST. MARY ELEMENTARY SCHOOL, MARION, OHIO

The mission of the St. Mary School Community is to provide foundations in the Catholic Faith and in academics that will enable our students to become individuals who value and live their faith and will be *lifelong learners* and problem solvers.

CENTERVILLE-ABINGTON COMMUNITY
SCHOOLS, CENTERVILLE, INDIANA

Centerville-Abington Community Schools, in partnership with families and the community, educates ALL individuals to be *lifelong learners* and responsible citizens in a global society.

STONEWALL JACKSON HIGH
SCHOOL, QUICKSBURG, VIRGINIA

At Stonewall Jackson High School, our mission is to equip students for *lifelong learning* through lessons in academics, accountability, and attitude.

Lifelong learning is the focus of many districts' policies on instructional practice and educational goals. But the truth is, just saying a district will promote lifelong learning in students is just not enough. Policy without guidelines is simply words on a paper, however good they sound.

Teachers really do want to promote lifelong learning. That is not the issue. The problem is that no one ever shared exactly what it means to be considered a lifelong learner. What's more, even with a definition in hand, how do teachers then make lifelong learning accessible to *all* students?

WHY AND HOW THIS BOOK FIRST CAME TO BE

Meet the Authors: Margie Pearse

I had the privilege of living in the district where I taught. Because of this, I got to see many of my students grow up around me. I began to notice something over the years: the students who valued learning and saw it as important in my class as sixth graders were the same students who experienced great success as adults. I discovered a pattern. These children, although coming from diverse backgrounds and family situations, all held common traits. I came to describe these commonalities as the qualities of a proficient lifelong learner.

I continued to study what I believed to be my proficient lifelong learners. I defined a proficient lifelong learner as someone who continued to be successful long after being in my classroom. I assessed their sense of well-being, zest for learning, academic achievement, ability to create goals and achieve those goals, willingness to be flexible and steadfast, and awareness of his or her responsibility toward others to be evidence of their success. I then turned to research.

Over the next ten years, I continued with my observation and research on what it takes to become a lifelong learner. I identified certain qualities that all proficient lifelong learners possess.

Lifelong learners share the following common qualities:

1. Lifelong learners are tenacious.
2. Lifelong learners are reflective.
3. Lifelong learners are metacognitive.
4. Lifelong learners are divergent thinkers.
5. Lifelong learners are self-efficacious.
6. Lifelong learners see learning as valuable.
7. Lifelong learners are collaborative.

I have always been a proponent of the idea that the best defense is a strong offense. I needed to broaden the focus of my teaching. Even more, if students are not aware of the qualities it takes to become a lifelong learner, their capacity to become one is obviously limited. I was back to the drawing board. What could I change in my instructional practices to instill these qualities in my students?

That was ten years ago. During that time, I tested hundreds of ways to promote the qualities of a lifelong learner. Little by little, my students began to embrace these qualities, and with the use of the ideas from this book, they began to use them more instinctively. I discovered that the qualities it takes to become a lifelong learner can be developed in all children, with proper guidance. This was ground-breaking information, and at that point I knew I needed to share it with as many teachers as possible.

The favorite ideas that are included in every chapter are the result of over ten years of trial and error, observation, and research. Every idea you will read is tried and true. They cross content area and grade level, infusing the qualities it takes to become a lifelong learner. They are also very "tweakable" to fit your unique circumstances in your classroom. I know this because I used most of them while coaching teachers from kindergarten to high school.

I then shared my discoveries on empowering all students with the qualities of a lifelong learner with a friend and well-respected administrator, Mary Dunwoody. I will let Mary take it from there.

WHY AND HOW THIS BOOK THEN CAME TO BE

Meet the Authors: Mary Dunwoody

I grew up in a home with a wonderful flower garden. These were not just any flowers, but beautiful roses. The roses were cultivated and nurtured lovingly, first by my grandfather and later by my father. As far back as I can recall, I wondered why some roses bloomed and blossomed to their fullest beauty, while others on the same bush would open, but never quite to their fullest potential. The care was the same, the position of the sun and shade identical—but the end product was markedly different. Even now, when I am fortunate enough to receive a flower arrangement, I watch carefully as each flower moves toward its full bloom, and just as I recall from many years ago, some completely blossom and others simply open.

As a teacher I often felt the same wonder: Why and how did some students achieve success and fulfill their goals, while others seemed content to meet only minimum potential? With a very broad range of experience, from nonpublic and private education classrooms to a public school district that struggles continuously to address the needs of students of poverty and low expectation, I saw students in classes in both arenas become highly successful as learners and, eventually, as adults in society. I was a determined teacher, focusing on individual strengths and needs to direct my instruction, and I knew intuitively that there are definite traits that would lead to greater success for my students.

As a principal, I dedicated time to providing research-based, best-practice techniques to my teachers, and I supported their efforts with ongoing training opportunities. Once again, as with my flower observations, I was baffled by the fact that so many of the students we served came from similar backgrounds of generational poverty and low academic expectation—and yet, here they were: all arriving at school, eager to learn, excited by the prospect of learning to read. But regardless of these optimistic starts, many of those students never seemed to blossom to their fullest beauty. However, there were always those remarkable students who were able to immerse themselves into the academic experiences offered to them and go on to solid success as adults. Clearly there are qualities, as identified in this book, that can be embedded into our curricula and the daily delivery of instruction. Once we own this treasury of knowledge, it is really incumbent on us as professionals to share these traits with our colleagues and provide some suggestions for their work.

When Margie invited me to partner with her in this endeavor, the offer could not have been more timely. I am in a new chapter in my own professional journey, and this collegial experience allows new opportunities for my own growth and passion to merge. The qualities of lifelong learning are the undeniable right of every learner, and our favorite ideas can be used immediately across grade levels and subject areas to allow students to access and master these traits for present and future use. Margie has brought her special brand of instructional expertise to my students and professional colleagues, and now, many readers will be able to benefit from her passion and talents, as well.

THE OBJECTIVE OF THIS BOOK

Given the incredible stresses the family is now experiencing, school has become a vital refuge for a growing number of children (Bernard 2005, 124). The classroom is more of a home to some children than where they live. Teachers see this every day. The school environment needs to be a place where students become well grounded. The qualities of a lifelong learner can fill in these gaps. It is critical for children to consciously understand that no matter what their interests are, no matter where life takes them, these qualities will enhance their capacity to excel. There is freedom, power, and responsibility in realizing that one can positively affect his or her future.

Our mission is to demystify the concept of what it takes to be a lifelong learner by making it as explicit and accessible as possible. Infusing the qualities of a lifelong learner into daily instruction provides the backdrop necessary to achieving life's greatest possibilities.

Our goal is to help *all* children reach their full potential. Empowering students with the qualities of a lifelong learner has long-lasting benefits. Students can be taught to think differently about their future by realizing they have a big part in shaping it. This book will prepare students with the information, competence, and unique qualities essential to succeed in a rapidly changing world.

Acknowledgments

We are very grateful to the following people who played a key role in making this book come about. First, a big thank-you goes out to Thomas Koerner, our publisher and vice president of Rowman and Littlefield Education. You believed in us from our very first conversation! You recognized the potential in this work and gave us the voice we needed to spread the message. To Carlie Wall: You are amazing! Thank you for your patience and guidance every step of the way. It was such a comfort knowing that you were just an email away. To Lindsey Schauer, thank you for your expertise in the details. We appreciate your guidance in pulling it all together. To Dr. Rina Vassallo: Thank you for your beautifully crafted foreword. You exemplify the qualities of a lifelong learner in all you do. You are a true inspiration! To Mary E. Dunwoody: Special thanks for sharing your time and technological talents with us. And last but certainly not least, thank you to the teachers and students at Southeast Delco School District, Springfield School District, Coatesville Area School District, Neumann University, and Cabrini College. Without you, many of the ideas in this book would not be considered so tried and true!

—Margie and Mary

I am forever thankful to God for His provisions. Never have I experienced such a deep sense of flow as when writing this book. To my soul mate, best friend, and husband, Chris: thank you for making all my dreams come true. To my children, Christopher, Drew, and Gloria: you bring such joy to my life. Your genuine interest in this work inspired me to push forward. I also want to thank my siblings, Linda, Joanne, Nancy, and Joe, and my lifetime friend, Mo. I love spending time with you! To my sweetheart, Ayden: You are my favorite little guy in the whole wide world. I am also grateful to all the wonderful teachers from Springfield School District and Coatesville Area School District, who made contributions to the book. Thank you for believing in me. Thank you to Matt Gauzza, Chris Pearse, and Gloria Pearse for all your patience, help at a moment's notice, and tech savvy. I am especially grateful for my dear friend and coauthor, Mary Dunwoody. It was a joy to work with you. Your gentle spirit kept me calm throughout the process. You are a gem!

—Margie

First of all, I thank my treasured family: my dearest friend and husband, Bill, and my extraordinary children, Mary, Brendan (and Nola), Sean (and Heather), Rory (and Emiko). You are my center and my inspiration. Your steadfast love gives me wings to fly and a warm nest for return. Thank you to my many professional colleagues whose hard work and unwavering belief in the potential of every learner provided guidance and substance to this work. And particular thanks to a true lifelong learner, my writing partner, Margie Pearse, for allowing me to work hand-in-hand and to share your contagious passion.

—Mary

Introduction

> The school that becomes a self-renewing enterprise will shape its own future.
>
> —Roland S. Barth

The implementation of the Common Core State Standards (CCSS) is a paradigm shift designed to advance our nation's educational system. The standards promote critical thinking skills and provide a common thread across states for curriculum design.

We applaud the adoption of the CCSS and celebrate the premise that common standards propose better opportunities for all students to get what they need out of school in order to succeed in an ever-changing, fast-paced, highly demanding world. Our gift presented through *Learning That Never Ends* is a way for all students to acquire what they need to navigate successfully, not only through the CCSS, but well beyond them—for life.

HOW TO USE THIS BOOK

Each chapter is written in a structured way. The format allows you to either focus on one topic in each chapter or simply read it through from cover to cover.

The chapters are structured in the following way:

1. Definition of the quality
2. Why the quality is important
3. What cognitive processes foster the quality
   • Favorite teaching ideas that cultivate those processes
4. What it takes to adopt that quality
   • Favorite teaching ideas that promote the use of the quality
5. How you can become a teacher who uses that quality in your practice

OUR ADVICE ON WHERE TO BEGIN

Introduce Each of the Qualities of a Lifelong Learner in a Short Anchor Lesson

We have found it worthwhile to begin the school year by introducing each of the qualities in an anchor lesson. We understand how busy the first few months are, but we highly recommend investing the hour it takes to teach the individual qualities to your students. By doing this, you will generate awareness, develop a common language unique to the qualities, and build a frame of reference to use throughout the year.

An anchor lesson also provides a safe way for students to try using the qualities in a structured environment, resulting in more automatic use and greater student transfer and application. In this way, Costa and Kallick emphasize that students will become more skillful in their use of the habits; they will recognize the habits' merits and values, use them more spontaneously in an increasingly wider set of situations, and become more self-evaluative in their use of them (Costa & Kallick 2009, 3).

What a Typical Anchor Lesson Might Look Like

If it is possible with your schedule, we recommend one lesson a week for the first seven weeks of school. Each lesson will take about thirty minutes, and the benefits are huge. We understand this may not be possible with some class schedules and content requirements. In this case, feel free to tweak the following anchor lesson to best fit your program.

1. Begin with an essential question around the quality you are teaching in order to pique interest and get students instantly engaged in the learning. Have students then Think/Pair/Share or Think/Write/Pair/Share.
   - A few examples of good questions for teaching "Lifelong learners are tenacious" might be, "What is one time that you felt like giving up, but you didn't?" Or "Who is someone that no matter what happens, he or she never gives up? Share what you know about that person." Or "'When the going gets tough, the tough get going.' What does this mean to you? Is it important in school? Out of school? Why? Why not?"
2. Name the quality you are teaching and define it.
3. Have small groups brainstorm when and where the quality would be most beneficial to use in and out of school.
4. Write a T-chart on paper with the following headings: What the quality looks like/What the quality sounds like. Give one to each small group. Provide three minutes for students to create a list of what it looks like and sounds like when the quality is being practiced.
5. Provide time to reflect on how students might use this quality in the next week.
6. Challenge students to pay attention to when they see the quality being used during the next few days. Check in with them later to find out.

Here are some great follow-up ideas that are useful throughout the year and take very little time:

- Ask questions that prompt students to use the qualities during projects, problem-solving, social issues, and so on.
- Ask students to become observers of when they see an exemplary use of the qualities. Take a few moments each week to share.
- Include qualities as criteria in rubrics.
- Share how using the qualities helped you in your life in some way.
- Ask students which qualities they use most frequently. Have them share examples.
- Ask students which qualities are the most difficult for them to use. Why do they think those qualities are difficult? What can they do about it?

- During long assignments and projects, share how using the qualities is helpful before, during, and after the process.
- Use real-life problems, and brainstorm what qualities would be most beneficial for creating a positive result.
- Model for students how to use each quality in the face of new challenges.
- As a debrief, have students reflect on what lifelong qualities are especially relevant to the lesson.
- Have students defend their use of the qualities in a project, a long-term assignment.
- Have students analyze characters in a story, novel, or film or from history or science through the lens of the qualities of a lifelong learner.

We have included one format for using the book. This is how we plan to use it with our teachers and student teachers. But please do not feel restricted by this format. This book is a gift to you. Use it any way that fits best.

ONE IDEA FOR USING THIS BOOK

Begin each chapter whenever you choose to introduce the quality. Read and understand the definition and why the quality is important to becoming a lifelong learner.

Using this information, teach an anchor lesson on the quality. See above for a sample anchor lesson format.

Read and understand what cognitive processes foster that quality. Incorporate the favorite teaching ideas provided.

Reinforce the automatic use of the quality by including some recommended follow-up activities in daily lessons. See above for a list of possible follow-up activities, but really the ideas are endless.

Read and understand the section on what it takes to develop the quality. Try out a few of the recommended teaching ideas.

Reflect on the effectiveness of any ideas you tried out with your students. Take notes in the margins accordingly.

Collaborate with colleagues who are either reading the book or are simply interested in promoting lifelong learners. Share ideas, take notes, and learn from each other and from your students.

Include more follow-up activities and favorite teaching ideas.

Read and understand how to become a teacher who uses that quality in his or her practice. Reflect on struggles and strengths. Make personal goals.

Repeat the steps above for each of the qualities.

Revisit each chapter to try new ideas or focus on a particular need.

Read the references for more books to read on the topic.

Each quality that unfolds in these chapters is truly a singular gift to you as well as to your students. Remember to nurture your lifelong learning needs too! As you choose and customize a particular quality, take time to savor it, grow it, and feel it bloom. Consider this book a springboard to continual personal and professional growth, and celebrate your willingness and desire to learn and grow, both professionally and personally!

1

Lifelong Learners Are Tenacious

Life is a grindstone. Whether it grinds us down or polishes us up depends on us.

—L. Thomas Holdcroft

WHAT IS BEING TENACIOUS?

The Merriam-Webster definition of *tenacious* is "persistent in maintaining, not easily pulled apart, tending to hold fast, unrelenting."

Being tenacious means having the capacity to survive, to progress through difficulty, to bounce back, to move on positively again and again in life (Gibbs 2006, 41). Tenacity means knowing that failing is a just a cue to try something else. Tenacious people are self-driven. They give a little extra because they know it will help get them where they want to go.

WHY IS TENACITY IMPORTANT
TO BECOMING A LIFELONG LEARNER?

Tenacious people do not give up easily. They stick to an activity until the end, having resolve and a strong work ethic. They accept that stress is a healthy part of everyday life and do not let life's problems take them down.

Stuff happens. Tenacious people recognize that no one is immune; pressure is simply a by-product of life. What counts, then, is not the amount or the kind of pressure we face—but the ways we come to deal with it. How you handle pressure can determine nothing less than how rewarding a life you'll lead (Garofalo 2008, 163). Lifelong learners summon the courage to try. They don't give up without a fight.

It is not the circumstances—it is what we choose to do in response to the situation that determines who we are and who we will become. Tenacity matters. Tenacious people look at mistakes and failures as a rough draft. They see the struggle as temporary and necessary to accomplish their goals. It is something to go through, not get around. Heart, soul, guts . . . these are the vital building blocks of tenacity.

> Nothing in this world can take the place of tenacity. Talent will not; nothing is more common than unsuccessful men with talent. Genius will not; unrewarded genius is almost a proverb. Education will not; the world is full of educated derelicts. Persistence and determination alone are omnipotent. The slogan "Press On" has solved and always will solve the problems of the human race.
>
> —Calvin Coolidge (1872–1933),
> thirtieth president of the United States

WHAT COGNITIVE PROCESS FOSTERS TENACITY?

Making Predictions

When we make predictions we become active participants, anticipating the direction of the learning (Beers 2003, 45). Predictions compel us. They keep us committed, and commitments build tenacity.

Predicting keeps us part of the action. There's a personal investment with every prediction made. Guessing is a childhood pleasure, but with the popularity of Fantasy Football, it is obvious that making predictions keeps even adults in the game.

Two of Our Favorite Ideas for Empowering Students to Predict

Quotation Mingle
1. Ahead of time, extract about eight interesting sentences from whatever your students will be learning about. Copy them onto index

cards and give one to each student (you will need to make three or four copies of each sentence).

2. Distribute the cards, and tell students to mingle around the room comparing their quotes to what others have. You may need to model what mingling looks like so students know to pause for a minute to talk to each person they greet. After sharing their quotes with each other, pairs should make predictions about what they will learn and read about today.
3. Allow students to continue mingling and predicting for about five minutes.
4. Call time. Students freeze and form pairs, and pairs form groups of four. In groups of four, students reach a consensus predicting the main idea of the reading to come.
5. Read the article. Students confirm and revise their original predictions (Daniels & Steineke 2011, 131; Beers 2003; Wilhelm 2002).

From Modeling to Independence: Making Predictions. It is essential for teachers across all grade levels in every subject area to model the strategy of making predictions. We cannot assume students understand how to make good predictions or why it is even important that we do it.

Below is a modeling lesson on how to gradually release the responsibility of making good predictions for emergent readers. The think-aloud strategy is particularly helpful in developing the implicit skills necessary for making predictions explicit to all students:

1. Think aloud before reading a book to students, modeling the process of predicting before reading. "I found an interesting book at the library and by looking at the cover I am guessing or predicting the story will be about _____ and _____. _____ about the text led me to make this prediction. When we use what we know to make a guess before we read, that is called 'predicting.'"
2. Think aloud while reading a book to students, modeling the process of predicting while reading. "Hmmm . . . my prediction that the story would be about _____ was right, but I did not think that _____ would happen. I'll make a new prediction that _____ will happen based on what we've read so far."

3. Think aloud after reading, modeling the process of reflecting on predictions after reading. "My first prediction was _____. After reading part of the story I predicted _____. Now that I am finished reading I think my predictions were close/not close to what really happened because _____."

As students move toward independent integration of the strategy, teachers should provide opportunities for them to make, revise, and verify their own predictions before, during, and after reading. Here are some suggestions:

- Preselect and mark stopping points throughout a book. Use sticky notes to mark students' books if they are reading independently.
- As a class or in groups, have students make and discuss predictions. Have them think aloud as they share their predictions. Always bring them back to what about the text led them to make that prediction.
- Have students write or draw predictions in journals, learning logs, or on chart paper to refer to throughout the story.
- At the preselected stopping points, have students refine, revise, and verify their predictions. Make changes to the journals or chart as needed.
- At the end of the story, have students reflect on their predictions in relation to the entire story, and ask them to draw a final sketch or write a learning log response about their predictions. Encourage students to think about why their prediction was correct or incorrect and what information they are using to make that decision. ("Predicting," n.d.)

WHAT DOES IT TAKE TO BE A TENACIOUS LEARNER?

Tenacious learners are determined even when it appears that something is too hard. They use that as motivation to take on the challenge and stay the course, even more. Being tenacious boils down to being willing to lay it on the line, give it your all, reach down deep, and with no holds barred, let the best that you have to offer fly (Sitomer 2008, 149).

Students need to understand that certain degrees of failure are to be expected, and when we teach our students to stay tenacious through it, we are safeguarding their quest to become lifelong learners. It is that kind of uncommon resolve that prepares students for the challenges in life.

What does it take to be a tenacious learner? We must be patient. Always giving in to our immediate desires can cloud our vision and get us off track. Tenacious learners exercise impulse control. They see the value in *delaying gratification*, and they have the strength to do it. To be tenacious means appreciating what it takes to *build the mental stamina* necessary to stay focused and achieve academic success. Tenacity takes gumption. *Having gumption* entails showing courage, determination, and resilience in the midst of difficulty.

Delaying Gratification

We live in a world where immediate results are expected; Facebook, texts, faxes, DIRECTV, and so on. Growing up in a culture where instant gratification is the norm can obviously influence our ability and willingness to show restraint.

Rome wasn't built in a day, right? We need to let students in on this. Think of what it takes to become a doctor: four years of college, four more years of medical school, and at least three years of residency. That's a minimum of eleven years of invested time to achieve a single goal. It is frightening at times to think how many American hospitals now recruit their residents from other countries. Are Americans so used to getting immediate results that we are not willing to put in the eleven years it takes to become a doctor? We hope not. In a culture that offers instant gratification at every turn, delaying gratification is a skill that must be cultivated, modeled, and practiced.

Tenacity depends upon students becoming more self-controlled and less impulsive. We need to deliberately build students' capacity for delayed gratification (Jackson 2011a, 75). Students need to understand that most learning involves some lag time between the energy invested up front and the benefits this effort will bring about (Garofalo 2008, 36).

For many of our students, the learned behavior when something goes wrong is to give up (Tileston 2010a, 25). Dan Goleman, author of *Emotional Intelligence: Why It Can Matter More Than IQ*, considers impulsivity to be the main reason students struggle with finishing a task. He concurs that teaching students how to delay gratification and stifle impulsiveness will increase their willingness and capability to accomplish goals in and out of school (Goleman 1995, 45).

To be honest, some tasks are boring. Gratification can come from completing something that is tedious, but which we know must get done. There is satisfaction in realizing you have the wherewithal to push through a wearisome task. Yes, we teachers strive to provide engaging lessons all the time. But, to be honest, life is not fun 100 percent of the time. Letting your students in on this is freeing. Show them how you manage the monotonous tasks in life and still follow through. They will be grateful. And every now and then, when your students complain about how boring something seems, remind them of the skills you used to push through the boredom to get the job done.

Some tasks are boring. Acknowledge this and share how you survive through it. Adults have to do tedious things every day. What about cleaning? That's not fun, but it's necessary. It is amazing how you can make any mundane chore doable. Share how you manage through it to completion. There is definitely some power in the old adage "Whistle while you work."

Life is not about taking the easy way out. We all have to make short-term sacrifices to benefit in the long term.

Rob Garofalo Jr., author of *A Winner by Any Standard*, offers ten practical suggestions to help students delay gratification:

1. Get most of your homework done before enjoying free time.
2. Get started in even the smallest way on a report or project the same day it's assigned.
3. Reserve your after-school time by getting in the habit of waking up half an hour earlier to get some work done on long-term assignments. This will free up time in the evening.
4. Put aside a little money from everything you earn. Be careful not to overspend.
5. Study little by little, far in advance of an exam.
6. Make moderation a habit—too much of anything is not good. Take some time for work, play, TV, computer, friends, and especially your family.
7. Don't wait to feel good about doing the right thing. Just do it. Act and your feelings will follow.

8. Give your strongest effort in school now, knowing it will all pay off down the road.
9. Be patient and believe in yourself. All good things take time. You have worked through tougher situations, and you can do the same this time too. Give your strongest effort in school now, knowing it will all pay off down the road.
10. Push your way through the awkwardness of beginning a new life habit. The payoff is huge! (Garofalo 2008, 25).

Two of Our Favorite Ideas for
Empowering Students to Delay Gratification

Oh, the Temptation! The Stanford Marshmallow Experiment indicates that good impulse control might be psychologically important for academic achievement and for success in adult life (Lehrer 2009). In this popular test, several children wrestle with waiting to eat one marshmallow in hopes of winning a bigger prize if they wait.

1. Share a little background about the Stanford Marshmallow Experiment, but don't give away the results.
2. Show the following video clip. It is adorable. See Igniter Media, "The Marshmallow Test," at http://www.youtube.com/watch?v=QX_oy9614HQ.
3. Have students notice what they see happening in the video. Share observations in small groups. Extend the conversation by asking why the children may have reacted differently to the challenge of eating either one marshmallow immediately or two later.
4. Then do the big reveal. Show and tell your students that Stanford actually followed the lives of those students in the marshmallow tests, and those who had the self-control and self-regulation skills were more successful and more fulfilled as adults.
5. Ahead of time, make and laminate bookmarks out of Garofalo's ten suggestions above (one for each student). Hand bookmarks out, read silently, and have small groups discuss them. You can use the following prompts as discussion starters:
   - Which suggestion do you think is the most important? Why?
   - Which suggestion are you best at already? Explain.

- Which suggestion is the hardest for you to accomplish? Why? What can you do about it?
- Which suggestion will you commit to trying in the next week? (Write it down in their agenda books, homework book, planner, something.)

6. Students keep bookmarks. Refer to them in class at appropriate times.
7. Check back with the class the following week and have students reflect on their progress.
8. Repeat steps 5–7 each week.

Accountability/Coaching Partners   Coaching partners are a way to encourage accountability. They are long-term partnerships. You form the partners by matching students who are compatible but range in ability. They can be utilized at any given point during the lesson and may meet to simply touch base or longer. It depends upon your purpose.

For younger students, coaching partners can be used in the following ways:

- Retelling
- Summarizing
- Connecting
- Brainstorming
- Echo reading
- Generating and answering questions
- Using manipulatives
- Problem-solving
- Experimenting
- Working in stations
- Discovering nature
- Paired reading
- Listening to books on tape
- Listening to each other

For the older student, a coaching partner can be an excellent resource when a specific project is being assigned. Here are just a few:

- Discussing ways to meet a deadline
- Reviewing and summarizing learning
- Creating working goals
- Problem solving
- Generating a formula
- Designing a working plan
- Reflecting on the progress of working goals
- Clarifying evaluation criteria on a rubric
- Reviewing each other's progress on a project
- Answering questions about a project
- Revising
- Doing peer reviews
- Brainstorming ideas
- Coming to a consensus
- Providing emotional support
- Prioritizing plans to complete something
- Listening
- Celebrating each other's successes

Building Mental Stamina

Mental stamina, the ability to remain focused on a task, is a vital component in life. It often determines success or failure. Mental toughness is the ability to will oneself through less-than-ideal conditions, whether it is a four-hour standardized test or a grueling football practice in the heat of an August afternoon.

What most people fail to understand is that mental stamina is something that has to be practiced and developed over time. To strengthen our ability to focus and maintain mental stamina, we have to be willing to sustain interest and attention and to exclude competing or distracting interests (Keene 2008, 26). And how do we that—regardless of what's going on?

Sam Horn, author of *ConZentrate: Get Focused and Pay Attention*, suggests the following three ideas that can help you concentrate better—no matter what.

- *Five More Rule.* If you are in the middle of a task and tempted to give up—just do five more. Read five more pages. Finish five more problems. Concentrate for five more minutes. Continuing to concentrate when your brain is tired is the key to stretching your attention span and building your mental stamina.

• *One Think at a Time.* Instead of telling our brains not to worry about something (which causes the brain to focus on the very thing it's not supposed to think about), assign it a single task with start-stop time parameters and give it your undivided attention. Chunk a long-term project into doable parts and focus only on one part at a time. Then, when you've accomplished that task, begin another doable chunk.

• *Conquer Procrastination.* Don't feel like concentrating? Are you putting off a task or project you're supposed to be working on? Next time you're about to postpone a responsibility ask yourself, "Don't I have to do this at some point? Do I want it done so it's not on my mind? Will it be any easier later?" Those three questions can give you the incentive to mentally apply yourself, because they bring you face to face with the fact that this task isn't going away, and delaying will only add to your guilt and make this onerous task occupy more of your mind and time (Horn 2012).

Two of Our Favorite Ideas for Empowering Students to Build Mental Stamina

Positive Self-Talk   You foster tenacity in students by teaching them to make use of positive self-talk while solving multifaceted problems. Whenever possible, demonstrate how you use positive self-talk as you work through difficult situations. Explicitly model what it looks like and sounds like to remain focused on a rigorous task. This will really help students recognize what it takes to mentally finish strong.

Maintaining Mental Stamina, Courtesy of Professional Baseball   Find two short video clips of pitchers on the mound in extremely stressful situations. One clip should present a pitcher who is beginning to fall apart on the mound, whereas the other clip should be a pitcher who seems flawless. Show the failing pitcher first. Have students discuss what the pitcher is probably thinking at the time, and encourage them to come up with ways they might utilize the power of positive self-talk to keep calm and remain focused in such a stressful situation. Students should write these ideas down for future use. No matter what is going on with the pitcher, he still has to remain focused somehow. Let them figure out how. Then show the "superstar." What do they think he is saying to himself to keep focused? Okay, now comes the powerful part. Ask the students how this is like taking a test, working through a difficult project, or completing anything complex? Push the thinking by empowering the students to realize that it takes mental stamina to remain focused through any problem (Pearse and Walton 2011, 17).

Having Gumption

Adversity shouldn't be a shock to students, and the gumption to bounce back (resiliency) should be a habit. The greatest ally students can have in this world is an unrelenting determination to bounce back from whatever curveballs life throws at them (Sitomer 2008, 25).

A person with gumption is resourceful, acknowledging that curveballs do have an upside. They make you unyielding and more confident in solving future challenges. Having gumption means trusting that what doesn't kill us only makes us stronger. Not only are we stronger emotionally, perhaps spiritually, at our broken places, but our understanding of the world and our place in it—our cognitive life—is often enriched by struggle (Keene 2008, 102).

Rob Garafalo, author of *A Winner by Any Standard*, suggests that we use our past struggles, times when it felt like the world was crumbling, to accurately evaluate new problems. He adds that answering the following questions, before allowing stress to take over, will provide the message that things sometimes are not as bad as they seem:

1. How did things turn out?
2. Did the worst I expected to happen ever happen?
3. Did I surprise myself by how I was able to handle the problem? How?
4. Did I learn something from the experience?

Remembering these answers has a way of helping us face adversity in the future. Reflecting on past successes can build our confidence when meeting new challenges (Garofalo 2008, 151).

In actuality, having the ability to bounce back after adversity is recognized by many hiring agencies as advantageous. For instance, NASA
rejected people with pure histories of success, when they were soliciting
applications for astronauts, and instead selected people who had had significant failures and bounced back from them (Dweck 2006, 29).

Two of Our Favorite Ideas for Empowering Students to Build Gumption

Positive Messages and You Are Not Alone   We recognize the importance of showing student work around the classroom. We do see
the power, however, in also displaying posters with positive messages,
especially when it comes to developing gumption in your students. In
fact, we post our favorite messages more than once in convenient places
where students spend most of their time. However, hanging messages on
the classroom walls without using them in a teaching moment is just not
enough to make an impact. We believe "taking these messages down from
the walls" and making them livable for students will generate the common
language it takes to be tenacious. Here is one example of how to use a
positive message as a teachable moment:

1. "Everything is hard before it is easy" (Jackson 2011a, 53). Let your
   students in on this fact. Learning something new can be challenging.
   Getting assignments and projects that seem daunting and unachiev-
   able is scary. That is natural. We all feel anguish when starting
   something difficult. Wasn't riding a bike hard at first? Reading?
   Playing an instrument? Then it became automatic with practice.
   There is freedom in remembering that every new thing was once
   difficult, but we got through it.

We have included some additional positive messages that advocate the
importance of having some gumption.

1. "When things go wrong, don't go with them."—Anonymous
2. "It is better to be 0 for 20 than 0 for 0."—Michael Levine
3. "It's hard to wring my hands when I am busy rolling up my
   sleeves."—Linda Geraci
4. "Make it work."—Tim Gunn

5. "Shoddiness is the slickest of slippery slopes."—Alan Sitomer
6. "If you don't have time to do it right, you must have time to do it over."—John Wooden
7. "To win, you've got to stay in the game."—Claude M. Bristol
8. "The road is long between conception and completion."—Wilbur Pierce
9. "There is no giant step that does it. It's a lot of little steps."—Peter Cohen
10. "Courage is being scared to death but saddling up anyway."—John Wayne

You Are Not Alone It is important that students understand that no matter what they face in life, they are not alone. We all face obstacles. The choice we always have, however, is how we behave in response to the struggles we undergo.

There are countless ways of sharing stories of how people met with adversity and came through it victoriously. You can incorporate these stories as part of reading/writing workshop or a history lesson, or you can offer short snippets for a motivating moment in any subject.

Here are some ideas that work well:

1. Use inspiring stories of historical figures, athletes, and contemporary celebrities who overcame obstacles. Despite the challenges they faced, each was able to make important contributions. You can use any of the following to find such examples:
   - M. E. Snodgrass, *Beating the Odds: A Teen Guide to 75 Superstars Who Overcame Adversity* (2008)
   - http://www.disabled-world.com
   - http://www.learningrx.com/famous-people-with-learning-disabilities.htm
   - http://www.darynkagan.com/overcoming_obstacles.html
   - http://www.realmentalhealth.com
2. Have students talk to the adults in their lives whom they respect and ask them to share a time in their life that was especially difficult and how they got through it. How did this struggle ultimately impact their life? What might they do differently? What did they

learn about themselves through it? What advice could they provide because of it? (Garofalo 2008, 138).

3. Share your own repeated attempts at doing something difficult, emphasizing qualities such as gumption and tenacity. This shows students that, even though you are an adult, you too have to push your way through certain things in life (Garofalo 2008, 150).

HOW CAN I BECOME A MORE TENACIOUS TEACHER?

Seeking Excellence in Your Students

What is excellence? In our mega fast-paced, disposable world, students often don't gain an understanding of what constitutes excellence. We, as teachers, must provide instruction that exemplifies excellence, being careful to place students just beyond their reach. Csikszentmihalyi refers to this as an optimal experience. It's that level of challenge just a little out of reach that draws students into the learning and holds their attention.

To demand excellence means providing a rigorous curriculum that promotes critical thinking. Rigor is not as much about the standards. It's about how you ask students to reach the standards. Rigor means pushing students to attempt new things with the full understanding that those challenges may be just outside their grasp (Keene 2008, 88).

When students learn to engage in rigorous thinking and inquiry, they learn how to manage and work through frustration to solve problems on their own. Rigorous instruction demands that students stretch and arrive at new understanding—their own understanding. A rigorous curriculum is not intended for the elite only. It is intended for all students. Rigorous instruction is within but at the outer edges of students' capabilities and helps them expand what they can do. Rigor is "in reach"—and that reach is different for every student in each grade level, and within each discipline (Jackson 2011b, 20).

Students will rise to the expectations you hold for them. In fact, they will appreciate that you believe in them enough to challenge them. They may be scared and will probably protest at first. Be patient but firm. Once your students realize that you have faith in their ability and that you are not providing a way out, they will come around. In fact, students often exceed your expectations.

Seeking Excellence in Yourself

It is impossible to expect excellence in our students unless we are also striving for excellence in ourselves. As instructional coaches, we often ask teachers, "Would you go to a doctor who doesn't know the most progressive treatments or cutting-edge procedures?" Well, teaching is a profession too, and we owe it to our students to stay abreast of the latest pedagogy and top-notch instructional practices.

We do understand and recognize the pressure on teachers today. But using that as an excuse to stop learning doesn't cut it. Our advice is to learn one thing new each month and give it a go. It's impossible to try everything all the time. That's how we burn out. Instead, set aside some time each week for professional growth and research. You can read an educational journal or new book, observe a teacher you highly respect, try a new activity you heard about, or revamp a unit to exemplify excellence. Then share what you learned with your students. They will respect the fact that you care enough to offer the best instruction available.

Be tenacious with every student. Yes, we know the students who challenge everything. We are more than familiar with the student who refuses to do work or doesn't see the point of it. Tenacity doesn't mean you see every student as perfect. It means you see the possibilities in every student. Tenacity is never giving up. Failure is not an option. It is about believing in *your* ability to reach all students. Tenacious teachers see demanding students as an opportunity, because they believe in their own capability to inspire.

PROVIDING THE SUPPORT FOR STUDENTS TO EXEMPLIFY EXCELLENCE

Anticipating Confusion

Teachers know the importance of setting both reasonable and rigorous expectations. Good lesson design and planning are critical for building a layered instruction that provides access to the learning for all students. It means taking steps to resolve possible trouble spots and common mistakes before we ever teach the lesson and putting in supports for students to mitigate these problems. This leads to less uncertainty, more confidence, and increased student success.

That does not mean we take away the chance to wrestle with complex concepts. All the same, we want to make sure the struggle is a positive one that results in gained understanding (Jackson 2009, 110).

Here are some worthwhile ideas that anticipate confusion and provide necessary support for students:

1. *Wrong versus Right.* Show a correct example and an incorrect example side by side. Make sure the incorrect one includes a common error. Show all the steps for both, and challenge partners to identify what went wrong and when it started to go wrong. Students love to find mistakes. The power comes in challenging students to understand why, when, and how the error occurred. Pretend the wrong example belongs to the principal or one of your grade partners. That makes it funny and more engaging.

2. *Advance Organizers.* Prepare a graphic organizer breaking down the more difficult concepts and processes into manageable chunks. This allows students to experience small successes, giving them the confidence they need to continue. It also provides a place for students to hold their thinking so they can refer to it later when things get more complicated. It's important to remember that nothing breeds success *like success.*

3. *Prep Sheets.* Allow students to prepare something ahead of time for either a test or an upcoming complex task. Model how to do this. What's important to include? How do you know it's important? Where would you find that important? What is not important? It is amazing how invested students become in summarizing and determining importance when their grades are on the line. Providing time to share with a partner or small group makes it even better, because now students are asked to synthesize and evaluate their learning. It is a good idea to allow time in class for students to begin their prep sheets. This way, you are there to provide support and feedback on the process.

4. *Study Sessions.* Offer before- or after-school sessions to either prepare for a test or preteach an upcoming lesson.

Some of Our Favorite Ideas for Supporting Students in Exemplifying Excellence

Scaffolding Let students know that while you have high expectations, you are going to show them how to meet or exceed those expectations successfully and make the challenges of learning attainable for all students.

You can ease the intellectual shock of rigorous learning experiences for students through proactive support and careful scaffolding (Jackson 2011b, 105). With the right scaffolding, you are giving all students a pathway to success in school. Scaffolding can mean many things, but the purpose is always the same: to level the playing field so every student can enter into the learning. Keep in mind that the end goal is for students to independently succeed in rigorous work. Provide enough scaffolding for success, and remove that scaffolding when students no longer need it (Fisher & Frey 2007).

Here are some examples of good scaffolding:

- Providing advance organizers to structure thinking
- Building a knowledge base so those students without sufficient background knowledge may enter the learning
- Frontloading academic vocabulary
- Including collaboration in your daily practice (Turn & Talk, Think-Pair-Share, etc.)
- Chunking projects into feasible parts and grading small portions at a time
- Thinking aloud how you navigate through the learning
- Offering explicit and meaningful feedback in a timely manner
- Sharing how you manage time effectively through long-term projects
- Creating flexible groups so students can move in and out of them according to their present needs
- Modeling the importance of taking pride in a finished product
- Crafting rubrics at the beginning of an assignment and showing students how to use them to achieve the grade they want

- Making time for students to create daily work goals and reflecting on those goals at the end of a work period
- Modeling how you get yourself back on track after a setback
- Building time for students to make concrete, detailed plans to complete a task or project
- Showing what it feels like to savor a challenge
- Offering short-term payoffs (e.g., two-question "quizzes" as a quick formative assessment)
- Displaying how a positive attitude can help get you back on track
- Reflecting on what it feels like to accomplish something

Allowing for Brain Breaks   Learning is hard stuff. Becoming tenacious students takes energy, and staying tenacious means concentrating that energy throughout the learning process. It is impossible for anyone to stay focused every day, all day. What's a teacher to do?

Students need mental breaks in order to remain tenacious and focused. Neurologist and middle school teacher Judy Willis says that if instruction doesn't change delivery every twenty minutes, dopamine levels significantly drop in the brain (Willis 2009, 37). Younger students need to change tasks or activities more often. Even older students will feel their minds begin to wander after fifteen minutes of the same thing. Clearly, then, when creating lessons, we need to build in short mental breaks so students can remain focused on the learning. What do these mental breaks look like?

Games   Games provide motivation for all students. They not only learn more when playing a game, but their participation in class and their motivation for learning increases. Boys especially are naturally motivated when a review is turned into a friendly competition (Tate 2009, 23).

The amount of incidental learning that goes on while playing games is powerful. We love to go around and just listen while students are fully engaged in discussing the concepts they are learning, all because it's a game. We recommend, however, using games in partners or small groups simply because more students are involved in the learning. Whole class games can appear engaging, but realistically the only person truly engaged is the one whose turn it is. The other twenty-five or so students are free to un-engage until it is their turn. In addition, when students are playing in small groups, you have the freedom to work with individual students or to go around and listen for inaccurate thinking, paying close attention to how this will guide your instruction.

Energizing Brain Breaks   Energizing brain breaks are one- or two-minute exercises that help keep students engaged. Exercises that cross the midline of the body are especially effective. You can find plenty of great energizing brain-break ideas at http://www.energizingbrainbreaks.com/.

Teambuilding Activities   Investing time in building a sense of team with your students is beneficial for many reasons. It is a crucial step in students' feeling connected enough to the group to become fully invested in one another and the learning. Team builders also make terrific brain breaks for students and should be used throughout the year. There are endless teambuilding resources available. Here are a few of our favorite places to look:

- http://tribes.com/
- http://www.responsiveclassroom.org/
- http://www.kaganonline.com/index.php

Quiet Brain Breaks   Sometimes your students just need a minute of quiet to reflect, gather their thoughts, reenergize, and refocus. Taking a moment out to relax and recharge is good for all of us. Quite honestly, if we don't provide these moments for students, they will more than likely take them anyway, and probably not at an opportune time.

There are endless ways to include quiet brain breaks. Here are just a few to provide for students:

- When you feel like you just can't focus anymore while reading, just take your eyes off the page for a minute, look around, take a deep breath, and get back into the reading again.
- When you feel stressed during a test, close your eyes for a minute, tell yourself you got through this before and can do it again. Open your eyes, stretch a bit, and get ready to refocus.
- When all of a sudden you realize you're not paying attention anymore and you may have zoned out for longer than you realize, shake off the cobwebs, blink your eyes a few times, straighten up, take a deep breath, and refocus.

LIFELONG LEARNERS ARE TENACIOUS

All the world is full of suffering. It is also full of overcoming.

—Helen Keller

These words by Helen Keller confirm why tenacity is an essential quality for a lifelong learner. We will all make mistakes. We will all fail at times. But we need to know how to get up again, stay tenacious, and bounce back. It is tenacity that builds up that kind of resilience.

Fostering tenacity in our students empowers them to take on the challenges of life with courage, confidence, and persistence.

2

Lifelong Learners Are Reflective

The real man smiles in trouble, gathers strength from distress, and grows brave by reflection.

—Thomas Paine

WHAT IS BEING REFLECTIVE?

The Merriam-Webster definition of *reflective* is "marked by or engaging in reflection—being thoughtful, deliberative, contemplative; to think quietly and calmly."

To be reflective means to mentally wander through where you have been and to try to make some sense of it (Costa & Kallick 2000, 61). It is being quiet enough to pay attention to what's really happening within or around you.

Reflective thinking is the "Crock-Pot of the mind. It encourages your thoughts to simmer until they're done. It takes a good experience and makes it a valuable experience" (Maxwell 2009, 73).

WHY IS REFLECTION IMPORTANT
TO BECOMING A LIFELONG LEARNER?

Reflection is a skill critical to doing well in a complex world of information and relationships (Gibbs 2006, 93). In spite of that, the pace of our culture does not encourage reflective thinking. Americans generally value action over calm deliberation, often at the expense of self-evaluation and personal growth. Nevertheless, even in the center of the madness, lifelong learners are capable of objectively stepping back, taking a moment to self-reflect, analyze problems at hand, and tackle challenges with thoughtful intention.

Reflection is one of the greatest contributors to our ability to positively alter our own thinking and behavior (Jackson 2009, 92). Reflective thinking clarifies the big picture. Lifelong learners appreciate the benefits reflection offers. Being reflective, they learn from their successes and failures, discover what they should try to repeat, and determine what they should change. By mentally visiting past situations, lifelong learners think with greater understanding (Maxwell 2009, 72).

WHAT COGNITIVE PROCESSES FOSTER REFLECTION?

Summarizing

Summarizing is restating the essence of a lesson in as few words as possible in a new, yet succinct way. Summarizing requires students to reflect on what is important by analyzing the information, organizing it in a way that captures the essential ideas, and stating it in their own words.

Effective summarizing is one of the most powerful skills students can cultivate (Marzano, Pickering, & Pollock 2001).

Two of Our Favorite Ideas for Empowering Students to Summarize

Chunk-Sum-Sketch
- Use this tool with a passage that is somewhat long and/or complex. Skim over a piece of text and decide how you would divide up the reading into manageable chunks. Model how to chunk a reading piece (by paragraph is an easy start). You can draw brackets outside the paragraph.
- Students will read the text silently, one chunk at a time. (When you model this, read it aloud.)
- Write in the bracket a short phrase that would help them summarize or remember what happens. The short phrase serves as a summary.

- Help students react to what they read by drawing a small sketch to further remind them of the major ideas. (An emoticon works great here—e.g., anxious faces to identify a conflict, etc.)
- Continue through the reading using the steps above (Fuhrken 2009, 48–49).

We include a graphic organizer to use as a scaffold to Chunk-Sum-Sketch in appendix A. We found it to be a great way to introduce the idea of summarizing when reading a long piece of text (see "Summarizing and Synthesizing the Reading: Graphic Organizer" in appendix A).

Three-Minute Pause The Three-Minute Pause provides an opportunity for students to pause, reflect on the concepts that have just been introduced, summarize what they have learned so far, make connections to prior knowledge, and seek clarification.

Display the following statements to prompt reflective thinking:

1. Summarize key points so far.
2. Add your own thoughts.
3. Pose clarifying questions.

How does it work?

1. *Summarize key points so far.* Instruct the students to get into small groups. Give them a total of three minutes for the entire process. First, they should stop and reflect on the key points of the lesson up to that point, summarize the main idea, and share their summaries.
2. *Add your own thoughts.* Next, the students consider prior knowledge and connections they made to the new information. Share in small groups.
3. *Pose clarifying questions.* Are there things that are still not clear? What questions come to mind about what you have learned so far? What do you think will happen next? What makes you say that?

The Three-Minute Pause is a perfect chance for students to pause and reflect on their understanding before you move on in the lesson. It's quick, simple, and worthwhile (R. Jones n.d.).

Synthesizing Synthesizing information is combining what you already know with what you have learned to make something new. Giving students the opportunity to synthesize generates a deeper understanding of what they are learning. Essentially, as students reflect on what's important, they interweave their thoughts to form a comprehensive perspective to make the whole greater than the sum of its parts (Zimmerman & Hutchins 2003, 129).

Two of Our Favorite Ideas for Empowering Students to Synthesize

Deal or No Deal Copy and cut out ten cardstock briefcases. Number them 1–10 and display them somewhere in the room. What you put in each briefcase is up to you. We have seen teachers include names of various occupations, characters from books or movies, famous historians and scientists, or places to go in the community. At some point during the lesson, when you want students to reflect and synthesize the understanding, have a student "open" one of the briefcases. Ask students to reflect on the learning by asking prompting questions like, "What would (name of book character or famous historian) think about what we learned so far? What makes you say that?" Or if you have occupations in the briefcases, you might ask, "How would a carpenter use what we are learning? What makes you say that?" Change the categories in the briefcases about once a month to keep it engaging. The options are endless (Beninghof 2010, 76–77).

"Top 10" List Students respond well whenever we ask them their opinion. The "Top 10" idea is a way to combine synthesizing and evaluating. After reading informational text, watching a DVD, or listening to direct instruction, challenge your students to create what they would consider to be the ten most important ideas from the learning. During a mini-lesson, you can also challenge your students to discover the top five things they notice you doing, to think critically. Then let them turn-and-talk, sharing their noticings. Follow with the whole class sharing, and create a list of the top five things that are important whenever you _____. (Fill in the blank with whatever you are modeling at the time.) (See appendix A for a reproducible.)

WHAT DOES IT TAKE TO BE A REFLECTIVE LEARNER?

Reflective thinking enables you to distance yourself from the intense emotions of a particularly good or bad experience and see them with fresh eyes. When you reflect, you are capable of putting any experience into perspective.

Becoming more reflective is a choice we make. It is a purposeful decision to reflect on an idea or concept, and that takes time (Keene 2008, 76). It takes more than maturity to become a reflective person. It commands a teachable spirit, one that is humble enough to admit we don't know all the answers.

To become more reflective, we must be open to learning. That means listening attentively to what life is trying to teach us. Reflection requires a sense of inner presence, regardless of the demands of life. It means digging deeper than what we see, hear, or think about on the surface. And that takes desire, skill, and practice.

For lifelong learners, self-reflection becomes a way of life. Every experience is recaptured in thought, mulled over, and evaluated. Every decision is met with thoughtful deliberation and questions. What is life teaching me, and am I willing to learn it? That answer is at the heart of reflection.

WHAT IS ACTIVE LISTENING?

If you want to be a reflective person, you have to be a good listener. And to be a good listener, you have to value reflection.

Active listening is listening attentively and intentionally. It is a way of responding to another person that furthers mutual respect and understanding. Listening shows appreciation. As R. Umbach affirms, "Nothing increases the respect and gratitude of one man for another more than when he is heard exactly and with interest."

Active listeners pay attention and reflect. They go beyond simply hearing what someone says. They care enough about the other person to process what is said and to reflect on the meaning from that person's perspective. Being able to listen effectively is a gift; it takes skill and practice to negotiate successfully through the intricacies of conversation.

We as teachers cannot assume children have had experience learning how to navigate efficiently as listeners. According to Costa and Kallick, we spend 55 percent of our lives listening, but listening is one of the least taught skills (Costa & Kallick 2009, 42).

If our desire is to empower students to become lifelong learners, we need to incorporate active listening skills within the framework of a good learning environment.

Active listening depends on:

- Acknowledging the person who is speaking with full attention and eye contact
- Withholding one's own comments, opinion, and need to talk at the time
- Paraphrasing key words to encourage the speaker and to let them know they have been heard
- Paying attention not only to the words but also to the feelings behind the words—and reflecting feelings when necessary (Gibbs 2006, 86).

How do we teach the skill of active listening? Have students generate a definition of active listening using the following steps.

1. What does active listening look like, sound like, and feel like? In her book, *Reaching All by Creating Tribes Learning Communities*, Jeanne Gibbs (2006) recommends using a three-column graphic organizer like the one in table 2.1. Have students brainstorm ideas for

Table 2.1

Agreement: What Is Active Listening?		
ACTIVE LISTENING LOOKS LIKE...	*ACTIVE LISTENING SOUNDS LIKE...*	*ACTIVE LISTENING FEELS LIKE...*
Heads facing each other	Talking one at a time	Great
Eye contact	Encouragement	I'm important
People nodding	Paraphrasing	People care
Smiling	Asking questions to clarify	I'm appreciated
Face shows emotion	Laughing	We're friends
Leaning forward	"Good idea!"	I'm smart
Responding	"Uh-huh"	I belong
	"Yes!"	I have something to contribute.

Source: Gibbs (2006, 92).

each column heading and come to an agreement on what it takes to be an active listener. Sample answers are included in italics.

2. Create a wall-sized poster to refer to and use whenever you need to reinforce and remind students about the importance of active listening. It is also a great way to notice and celebrate active listening in the classroom as it happens.

3. Use probing questions to help students reflect on the importance of active listening:
   - How can you tell when someone is a really good listener?
   - How can you tell when someone is not listening to you? What are your feelings when that happens?
   - Why is it important to become a good listener?
   - What can you do to be a better listener?
   - What are some things you do to help you get back to listening to someone?
   - What things distract you the most when you are trying to listen to someone? What can you do to get back to listening when this happens?
   - When is it especially important to be a really good listener? (Costa & Kallick 2009, 42)

We need to spend time modeling for students how to bring the above descriptors to life. It is also helpful for students to see what "fake listening" is. Believe us—they know what you're talking about. One idea is to use the same graphic organizer above, but change the title to "Agreement: What Is Fake Listening?" This time, you model fake listening with either a willing student or another teacher (getting the principal to volunteer would be fun). Challenge students to notice what fake listening looks, sounds, and feels like from your dramatization (remember to include your cell phone). Then follow up with probing questions similar to the ones asked in step 3 above. This time ask students how it feels when someone is not listening to them.

With so many forms of communication available, you might think fake listening would be nonexistent. However, we know the opposite has occurred. Giving undivided attention seems to be a thing of the past. People just cannot be completely present when they are having so many conversations—be it tweets, emails, and words all at the same time. You can't really be listening to anyone this way, not even yourself. We may be the only people in our students' lives who can recapture what it means to give someone your undivided attention.

Two of Our Favorite Ideas for Empowering Students to Actively Listen

Teaching Paraphrasing

1. Have students form pairs and number off, #1 and #2.
2. Demonstrate how to paraphrase a statement.
   - Include some paraphrasing prompts like, "I think I hear you saying . . ." "Let me see if I got this right: . . ." "You would really like to . . ." "It is important to you that . . ." "You feel . . . when . . ."
3. Provide a discussion topic. This can be content related, a summary of the learning so far, an essential question, a synthesis, or a classroom matter.
4. Ask partner #1 to speak briefly on the topic (using a timer helps). Partner #2 listens and paraphrases what he or she heard. When time is up, let them switch roles.
5. Gather the whole class and generate a class definition for paraphrasing. Create a poster with a T-chart of "What paraphrasing is" and "What paraphrasing is not." Keep this visible for students to use as a resource. Ask students, "What is important about paraphrasing?" (Gibbs 2006, 350).

Taking Turns

Taking turns may seem obvious and even juvenile to bring up, but without a sense of order during class discussions, one or two students can monopolize the conversation, leaving others out. Teachers can be creative in making sure all students have a voice:

- Provide lots of opportunity to collaborate. It is easier to talk and listen in small groups.
- Distribute talking chips. When small groups are discussing a topic, each member is limited in how many times he or she can talk by the number of chips you give out. Each time a student makes a contribution, he or she must put a chip at the center of the table. Once a student's chips are spent, the student is forced to listen only. It is also

helpful to insist that everyone must participate in the conversation by saying that all students must contribute at least one chip.

- Use an object that can be passed from student to student. A student has control of the conversation when he or she has the "talking object," while everyone else must listen.
- Incorporate a social aspect by providing a conversation prompt and allowing your students to mingle around the room to get different perspectives on the topic. Students then return and write a reflection on something they learned from others.
- Take a "talk walk." Partner students up, give each pair a purpose, and tell them to go on a two-minute talk walk down the hall. When they come back, ask them to quietly reflect in writing what they learned from the conversation.

WHAT ROLE DOES SILENCE PLAY IN BEING REFLECTIVE?

"Silent and listen are spelled with the same letters." We love this quote and have really grown to appreciate the role silence plays when reflecting—that is, if we allow it. Silence is uncomfortable. We say we want just a minute of peace and quiet, and then when it comes, we often quickly fill it with some type of noise or activity. When we do that, we sometimes lose the lessons that come in the stillness of a silent moment.

Staying busy and connected is highly regarded. Silence doesn't really fit in our society, and yet we yearn for it. Why do you think retreats are such a booming business in America? We are convinced we need to go away to reflect. Doesn't that sound like an oxymoron? It's funny when you reflect on it. We find it novel to take time to listen to our own thoughts. I wonder what impact we can have on our future if we inspire our students to be still, pay attention to the silence, and know that wisdom can so often be found there.

Ellin Keene recognizes the untapped power of silence when she says, "To take time in silence, to hold an idea in our mind, to reflect over time—this is how understanding happens in our lives" (Keene 2008, 78).

As teachers, we want to let students in on what it means to get still, reflect on an idea, and ponder its significance. In these moments, students learn to search within for answers and dwell in ideas enough to explore their own intellect (Keene 2008, 97). The silence and pauses along the way allow for listening with empathy, for accessing background knowledge, and for formulating a response with precision and accuracy (Costa & Kallick 2009, 24).

How can we get students to see silence as valuable? Model it often. Show students what it looks like to be silent for a moment, right in the middle of your instruction, as you contemplate and prepare a thoughtful response. Reflect out loud, making sure silence is part of the deliberation. Yes, this will feel odd at first, but teaching students to get silent enough to listen to their own hearts and minds is influential in their becoming lifelong learners.

Two of Our Favorite Ideas for Empowering Students to Use Silence as a Tool to Reflect

Wait Time   Provide plenty of quiet moments to foster critical thinking. Let students in on the value of "wait time." Give at least three seconds of thinking time after a question and after an initial response. Wait three seconds before asking a question to increase anticipation and to illustrate the importance of the question to come (Gibbs 2006, 155). Model how you use wait time before responding to a student's question. Stop in the middle of your own question, get silent, look pensive, and share how you want to pay attention to the lessons you are supposed to be learning and how silence can bring those lessons to you.

Here are just a few of the benefits of wait time:

1. The length of student responses increases 400 to 800 percent.
2. The number of unsolicited but appropriate responses increases.
3. Failure to respond decreases.
4. Student confidence increases.
5. Students ask more questions.
6. Student achievement increases significantly. ("Levels of Questioning Bloom's Taxonomy" n.d.)

Using Silence for Transition Times   1. *Silence is golden.* A dear friend and excellent teacher, Tina Quiram, shares how her school uses silence to transition students from recess to learning:

I use "silence is golden time" every day right after recess, before I start my LA block. The children come in from recess and find a quiet place where they can relax and regroup for ten minutes. They take this time to get rid of their "recess self" and get their "LA self" ready for learning. Children can read, draw, write, or just sit quietly and reflect. It is not a time for talking—it is their time alone. As an added relaxation technique, I dim the lights and even add scented candles. The children really value this time. On some days if a change in schedule doesn't allow this "silence is golden time," the children are very disappointed!

2. *Passing time.* Make several copies of a clock face and glue each one to the front of a folder. Stick one question inside each folder. Place the clocks around the doorjamb so they are visible. As students are transitioning from your class to another or from one activity to another, open one up and read the question. Encourage students to "pass the time" thinking silently about the answer to the question. When students have successfully and silently transitioned, ask them to share their thinking with a partner. Change the questions every few weeks (Beninghof 2010, 47).

WHY PRACTICE SELF-REFLECTION?

Self-reflection is the opportunity to mull over an experience and evaluate it. It is essential for students to reflect on their progress in mastering content. It is, however, even more valuable when we provide moments for students to reflect on their ability to follow through, manage their time, and act in ways that are conducive to learning.

Self-reflection involves three components:

1. Experiencing events over again in the mind and in the heart.
2. Attaching emotions and thoughts to those experiences.
3. Reexamining and reevaluating how we feel and think, for future use.

Giving students ample time to self-reflect on their understanding empowers them to become lifelong learners. Self-reflection provides decisive feedback. Valuable learning may be lost if we do not give students the time they need to self-reflect. When students self-reflect, they gain ownership of their thinking because they know what they understand and what they don't—and ownership of thinking is crucial if one is to become a lifelong learner.

Are students headed in a direction that helps them fulfill their commitments, maintain their priorities, and realize their dreams? They need to know the answer to this question (Maxwell 2009, 19).

Two of Our Favorite Ideas for Empowering Students to Cultivate Self-Reflection

In-Class Journaling   In his book *Writing to Learn*, William Zinsser states, "Writing is how we think our way into a subject and make it our own" (Zinsser 1988). Journaling facilitates self-reflection and synthesis. It is a concrete way to show student thinking, which enhances self-reflective moments. Student journaling shifts the responsibility for learning away from the teacher and toward the students by encouraging self-reflection.

Through reflective journals; concepts, connections, and visual representations merge as students make learning their own. While writing, ideas become clearer, and students are more apt to discover the concepts being presented.

Reflective journals should include questions, prompts, sentence stems, essential understandings, problems, and open-ended prompts around both the content being learned and the personal skills it takes to succeed in academics and in life.

Some effective journal sentence stems are listed below. Students can choose from the list, or you can give them a specific prompt to reflect on and write about:

1. Ideas to remember about . . . are . . .
2. Reflecting on last night's homework: The problems I had the most trouble with last night were . . . because . . .
3. WILT logs (can represent "What I Learned Today" "What I Liked Today" and "Words I Learned Today")
4. What mistake did I make that taught me something about myself? What will I do differently?
5. What skills do I have today that I didn't have yesterday?
6. What have I done well this week? How do I know I did it well? How can I continue?

7. What was difficult for me in this lesson? What did I do to get through it?
8. What are some questions I still have about the learning today? Where might I find these answers?
9. When I am stuck in the middle of the lesson, what are some things I think about to get unstuck?
10. What is something I learned that amazed me? Why was it amazing?
11. What is something I learned that surprised me? Why was it surprising?
12. What was the most important idea I learned today? Why do I think it was the most important?
13. What connections can I make about . . . ? How does this help me understand the learning better?
14. What do I predict will happen with . . . ? Why do I think that?
15. How does what I learned today connect to yesterday's lesson? What do I think I will learn about tomorrow?
16. How can I create a visual representation of . . . and explain it?
17. What is my opinion about . . . ? What can I use to support my opinion?
18. How might I summarize the lesson in twenty words?
19. If I had to teach the lesson to a younger student, how might I explain it?
20. Where else would I use the information I learned about today?
21. What careers would most likely need or want the information I learned about today?

Yesterday Journals Yesterday journals are very influential in promoting reflective thinking. Students are required to reflect on their yesterdays in writing. They can complete entries either early in the morning at home or first thing when they get to class.

We assign them for a twenty-one-day period, because of the old saying "Twenty-one days makes a habit," and then students can decide whether or not to continue. It is always amazing how many students continue. In fact, several students suggested we write back, and so we did, creating something the students called "Reflections and Conversations of Yesterday."

Students decorated the front cover of a copybook, and we pasted on a list of possible prompts for them to use:

- What was the best part of my day yesterday? Why was it the best part?
- What was my biggest struggle from yesterday? How did I handle it? What might I do differently next time?
- What is something I am most proud of yesterday?
- How did I show my best effort yesterday?
- What is one thing I am especially proud of doing or saying yesterday?
- Was I a good friend yesterday? How can I tell?
- Was I a good sister/brother or son/daughter yesterday? How can I tell?
- What lesson did I learn yesterday that will help me grow as an individual? How can I apply that lesson again?
- What happened yesterday that needs more thinking time?
- How did I lead by example yesterday?
- What surprised me about yesterday?
- How did I show respect yesterday?
- How was I kind yesterday?
- What did I learn about myself yesterday either in or out of school?
- What is something I wish I said yesterday but didn't? What can I do about it today?
- How was I helpful yesterday?
- How did I show I care about working hard yesterday?
- What is something I would like to change about myself from yesterday? What can I learn from it?
- What qualities of a lifelong learner did I use yesterday?
- What is something I wish someone had noticed about me yesterday?
- What quality of a lifelong learner did I forget to use yesterday? How might using this quality have impacted the situation in a positive way?
- What is a goal I accomplished yesterday? What is a new goal I can make for today?
- How did I do on my plan for completing my project yesterday? What are my goals for today?

SELF-ASSESSING UNDERSTANDING

Self-assessment places the responsibility to understand on the student—and isn't that what learning is all about? Unfortunately, right now, there are way too many passive learners out there. Self-assessment empowers them to pursue learning.

Here are some fun and worthwhile ways for students to self-assess their understanding:

1. What's your windshield like? If your understanding were a windshield, how might it look? Clear? Streaky? Muddy? Explain your answer and make a plan how you can begin to spray-clean that windshield.
2. Paint color strips: Go to any home repair or paint store and pick up three-color paint strips. They naturally go from light to dark. Have students choose their favorite colors and use them as a self-assessment tool. As your lesson progresses, stop and ask your students to point to where their understanding is so far. Light—totally get it; middle—kind of get, but may need a little clarification; Dark—no clue. This will help you revise your teaching, form small groups, and confer with students. It also teaches students to be proactive learners and fight for understanding.
3. Hot glue the bottoms of a red and green plastic cup together. Place them at the center of small groups when they are problem solving. Together, they assess their understanding and decide to put the green cup up if they are moving along smoothly and the red cup up if they are confused and might need help. It is important to implement "Ask three before me" here, so you don't have red cups up every time one group member has a problem.
4. Thumbs up, thumbs in the middle, and thumbs down. This is a great choice for when students are sitting together on the rug or are in centers or stations around the room.
5. Place a traffic light card on each desk. As a formative assessment, have students point to where their understanding is according to red, green, or yellow.
6. On an assignment or exit ticket, students can write a 1: could teach it; 2: kinda know it; or 3: no clue still and need help.

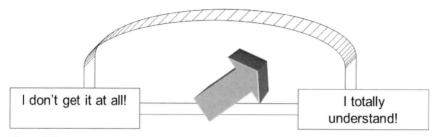

I don't get it at all!   I totally understand!

Figure 2.1

7. Make a copy of the personal meter in figure 2.1 for each student. Attach an arrow using a brad. Give these out so students have access to them throughout the lesson. Whenever you want to formatively assess the learning, have students stop and place the arrow where they believe their understanding is at that point. Quickly circulate the room as a way to measure how to proceed from there. At the end of the lesson, have students rate their understanding again. Students should create some evidence of their learning and hand it in as an exit ticket (Beninghof 2006, 34–35).

8. Have the students fill out a sheet that summarizes their understanding of today's learning objective and signals their efforts to reach the goals for the day's lesson. (See several sample forms in appendix A).

HOW CAN I BECOME A MORE REFLECTIVE TEACHER? BEING A REFLECTIVE PRACTITIONER

There is an interesting quote from the novel *Cutting for Stone*, by Abraham Verghese, which best represents our feelings on being a reflective practitioner: "The unexamined practice is not worth practicing." We believe it is crucial for teachers to reflect on the effectiveness of their instruction. To be honest, we really can't expect students to take reflection seriously if we don't practice it ourselves. Children catch on pretty quickly to the "Do as I say, not as I do" rule.

Critical reflection is about challenging and testing out what you do as a teacher and being prepared to act on the results (Crawley 2005, 167). Becoming a reflective practitioner takes time and effort. It means you are willing to pause enough in your planning and delivery to reflect on whether or not it is working, and if it isn't, you will do something to change it. It takes flexibility and confidence to become a reflective practitioner. It entails fervently searching for new trends in education, cutting-edge pedagogy, and creative instructional practices.

A teacher who values reflection consistently questions his or her practice and pedagogy by asking the following questions up front in the planning stages and again after the lesson has been delivered:

- Before the lesson: What is the purpose of my lesson? After the lesson: Did my students meet the objective? According to the answer: What will I do next?
- Before the lesson: How can I make this lesson relevant? After the lesson: Do the students know how what they learned relates to their everyday lives? If not, what will I do about that?
- Before the lesson: How will I engage my students in a meaningful way? After the lesson: Were all my students engaged in the learning? What was going on when I had the most engagement? Where in the lesson did I lose a few students' attention? Why is that? What can I do about it?
- Do my students know I care? How do I know?
- Do my students feel like they have a voice in the classroom? How can I tell?
- Before the lesson: How can I include the qualities of a lifelong learner in the lesson? After the lesson: Did students understand how using these qualities improves their learning? How can I make that more explicit in my teaching?
- Do the students care? If not, what can I do to help them to see learning as valuable?
- Before the lesson: What new strategies and activities can I try out? After the lesson: How did they work out? What activity should I considered a "keeper?" What didn't work out? Why? What can I do about that?
- Before the learning: How can I differentiate the instruction to meet the needs of all my students? After the lesson: How did I differentiate? Was it effective? If not, how can I improve?
- Before the lesson: How can I vary the delivery? After the lesson: Did I use enough modalities to meet the students' needs? If not, what could I do differently?

Model how you use reflection in your professional life. Share with your students what you are reading about professionally. Whenever you are trying something new, let students in on it, and ask what they thought about it afterward. Show students you are listening to them by asking for their recommendations and using them.

Survey students quarterly; asking them what they think of the class, your instruction, and how they measure their growth as learners because of it. Respect their suggestions, and let them know you appreciate their input. When you do this, you are a living example of someone who values reflection. That alone will make a great impact, because your students will understand that you care enough about them to give them a voice and that their voice is heard.

TAKING THE TIME TO DEBRIEF THE LEARNING

When we set aside time to debrief the learning, we are actually nurturing and promoting all the qualities of a lifelong learner. Permitting students ample time to remember, reflect, and revise their learning provides a tremendous opportunity for growth.

Richard Allington explains that the debrief is a teacher's opportunity to have students "identify points of confusion and levels of certainty" (Allington 2006, 114). Unfortunately, debriefing time tends to be the first thing to go when time is short. Yet, if you craft the debrief with care, the time spent can be minimal yet very powerful.

Shelley Harwayne argues that students need to "learn to pause, let things in their lives matter, hold their lives in their hands and reflect upon them" (Harwayne 1992, 93).

AN HONEST SELF-ASSESSMENT AND
A WILLINGNESS TO CHANGE AND GROW

We asked twenty teachers whom we consider exemplary what is critical to becoming a lifelong learner. It was amazing: Every one expressed the same advice. Be honest with yourself. Know when you need a change and be prepared to do the work necessary to create that change in a positive way. Be humble. Ask colleagues for honest feedback. Reflect on it, and then put it into action. Good advice.

Sometimes we are moved to another grade, a different subject, or even a separate school. What is our first reaction? We freak out. We don't want this change. We fight it tooth and nail. We like uniformity, but that is not where we do our best growing. At one time or another, every one of the twenty teachers was moved to another teaching position without any notice. What did they do? They used it to grow and become better. Yes, it was scary. Yes, they didn't want the change—but they took it with grace, seized the challenge, paid attention to the growth opportunities, and came out of it much stronger teachers and well-respected colleagues. It is in the uncomfortable places where we are forced to get real with ourselves and recognize it's now or never. Their advice: Let it be now. Be transparent. Use reflection to point out where you need changing, and change.

LIFELONG LEARNERS ARE REFLECTIVE

> Experience is a jewel, and it had need be so, for it is often purchased at an infinite rate.
>
> —William Shakespeare

Experience alone does not add value to a life. It's the insight people gain because of that experience. Reflective thinking is the place where experience becomes insight (Costa & Kallick 2009, 130).

Lifelong learners find time to deliberate on the day's experiences and are open to the lessons these experiences provide. They find comfort in the quietness of reflection and understand its potential for learning.

3

Lifelong Learners Are Metacognitive

Introduce students to the life of their minds.

—Ellin Keene

WHAT IS METACOGNITION?

The Merriam-Webster definition of *metacognition* is "an awareness or analysis of one's own learning or thinking processes."

Metacognition literally means thinking about thinking. It is thinking with intention, becoming more aware of the thoughts that run through the mind, and paying particular consideration to how those thoughts impact both personal and academic growth.

WHY IS METACOGNITION IMPORTANT TO BECOMING A LIFELONG LEARNER?

John Maxwell ascertains that what we think determines who we are, and who we are determines what we do (Maxwell 2009, 36). We now know, through research, that we have the power to control our thoughts. We are driven by them, so it is crucial that we listen to our minds, determine the direction our thoughts are leading us, and use metacognition to maintain focus in order to impact our lives and thus the lives of others.

It is the metacognitive system that makes decisions about what to do when problems with a task are encountered and pushes us to complete it task (Tileston 2010a, 24). Metacognition allows us to self-reflect, assess, and direct our own learning in and out of school.

WHAT COGNITIVE PROCESSES FOSTER METACOGNITIVE THINKING?

1. Monitoring and Repairing Your Comprehension

When we *monitor* our comprehension, we pay attention to whether or not we understand what we are reading, hearing, seeing, or saying. We pay attention to the construction of meaning. Students need to have these inner conversations, listening to that voice in their head speaking as they interact with the learning; it allows them to construct meaning. If the inner conversation is missing, students typically have no idea when meaning has been lost or understanding has broken down.

When we *repair* our understanding, we figure out what to do to make meaning when we are confused or lose our concentration. We fix what has broken down through the use of fix-up strategies. The initial and most important fix-up strategy of all is to cultivate awareness for when and how understanding waivers. Someone with strong metacognitive skills employs appropriate fix-up strategies immediately.

What Are the Fix-Up Tools Metacognitive Learners Use If They Do Not Understand?

- Make predictions before, during, and after the learning.
- Read or look ahead to clarify meaning, pausing and revisiting original predictions.
- Slow down if confusion occurs.
- Go back and reread. Sometimes that's enough.
- Take time to share with a partner.
- Identify what it is you don't understand.
- Do a quick summary before continuing.
- Seek help from an outside source.
- Use "positive self-talk," maintaining the stamina necessary to stay focused.

- Connect the learning to something personal.
- Connect the learning to something you learned at another time.
- Try to get a picture in your mind.
- Ask questions before, during, and after the learning.
- Have a conversation with the author, and write your part of the conversation in the margins of the text.
- Talk to the text and talk *about* the text.
- Take a quick brain break and get yourself back into the reading.
- Make inferences. This may mean identifying patterns of thought and relationships.
- Recognize when the inner conversation stops, and take the time to get your mind back on track (Pearse & Walton 2011, 11–12).

Two of Our Favorite Ideas for Empowering Students to Monitor and Repair Their Comprehension

Emoticons *Emoticon* is a fusion word for *emotion* and *icon* (e.g., a smiley face). Because of their link to popular culture, these symbols are enticing to students of all ages. They also boost engagement (Beninghof 2010, 29–30).

- Make a copy of the emoticons for each student. (Probably four or five different ones are plenty.) Go to http://www.getsmileyface.com/ for some options.
- Write the word "emoticon" on the board and display a few, asking students to describe the emotion that each symbol might represent. Write the descriptive words next to the symbol (e.g., confused, surprised, serious, happy, etc.).
- Distribute the emoticons and double-stick tape. Have each student stick the symbols to the inside cover of whatever book or reading material you are reading at the time. (For some reason, kids just love double-stick tape—it's novel, and that alone helps with interest—goofy, but true.)
- Ask students to use these emoticons to actively read, identifying places where they were surprised, still have questions, realize the importance, feel a connection, and so on.
- Have students pay particular attention when they have not used any of the emoticons when reading. Ask them what they think that means,

and challenge them to listen closely to their minds at work while reading. If they are no longer making any connections, they are not thinking and must get back on track.

- Use highlighter tape as an alternative to the emoticons for older students. Make a three-column index card for each student. (See sample in table 3.1.) Assign a color tape for each strategy, and put five strips in each column (roll up one side a bit so it easier to pick up). (See appendix B for a reproducible.)
- Extend the highlighter tape to the twenty-four-hour principle. It has been proven that we remember much more of what we learn when we revisit that learning within twenty-four hours. Using the active reading card in table 3.1, have students read their assigned text; then within twenty-four hours, students revisit where they placed their highlighter tape. Students record these reactions and responses in a Twenty-Four-Hour Principle Journal (see appendix B for the Twenty-Four-Hour Principle: Readers' Notebook and an extended version for high school/college students called Speed Dating and Metacognition).

Monitoring and Repairing Your Comprehension with Tiny Sticky Notes   Have students prepare little flag sticky notes with the following symbols: +, −, ?, and !. Each person should have several of each. Prepare a poster like the one in table 3.2. You can also make an index card for each student to keep for use independently and at home. They can keep their flag sticky notes right on the index card for easy access. While the students read, they use the symbols to hold their thinking.

Table 3.1

Determining Importance V.I.P.s (Very Important Points)	Questioning	Making Connections
Facts I think are most important . . .	Questions I have about the reading . . . *(Place three strips of different color tape in each column and curl up one of the sides for easy removal)*	Connections I made . . .

Table 3.2

SYMBOLS	WHAT THINKING THEY REPRESENT
+	V.I.P. (Very Important Point) Or confirms what you already knew. "I knew that!"
–	Contradicts what you thought. "I thought differently."
?	Confuses me. "I don't understand this." Or "I have a question about this."
!	Something new. An aha moment. "I didn't know that!"

Have students share with a partner the metacognitive strategies they used while reading and discuss the thinking behind how using these strategies helped them better understand the text. Clarify any misunderstandings as a whole class, post questions on a classroom "parking lot" area, or simply write "Questions for Further Discovery" on the board and let these questions be fuel for further discussion.

Take time for students to self-assess their active reading ability. Point out to students that if they have not used any flags at all while reading, it may be an indication that they are just fake reading and not really comprehending. Use this as a teachable moment. A think aloud would work well here, modeling how you monitor and repair your understanding as you read.

2. Making Connections

Making connections is the foundation for metacognition. Anytime we are presented with new learning or new tasks, the brain looks for existing connections in the brain. We can only uncover something new by connecting it to something we already know. The more connections the brain makes, the thicker the myelin sheath becomes. The thicker myelin sheath strengthens the neural pathway, which makes the new information more accessible for future retrieval (Sprenger 2005).

Connecting new learning to what we already know and understand is one of the most important tactics for helping students succeed. One of the things brain researchers are sure of is that if the brain is to move new information into long-term memory, it must be able to connect that new information to data it has previously stored.

If students don't have the personal background to recognize a connection to the content, we as teachers must work to create the context. It's not a luxury to be considered only if time allows: "Providing the context can be the difference between function and dysfunction in the classroom" (Wormeli 2009).

Two of Our Favorite Ideas for
Empowering Students to Make Connections

Tableaux Vivants (Living Pictures)   Tableaux Vivants are the perfect setup for small groups to share what connections they made during reading. It consists of bringing the information to life by creating and sharing scenes from the learning.

Here are the group directions for tableaux vivants:

1. Select an important event or idea from an article/chapter, a historical event, a newsworthy science moment, and so on.
2. Decide on characters, settings, and other details needed to create a living picture for the event.
3. As a group, decide how best to present the scene. One member of the group may narrate while the rest of the members form a motionless, silent scene.
4. For each scene, group members will create a "frozen image" while one member narrates. After you hold the scene for several moments, "melt" or move to set up the next scene. (We observed a teacher do this differently. Before moving to the next scene, he allowed each student to come alive for a moment and share his or her part of the scene and how it was integral to the chapter or book.)
5. Once everyone is in place, "freeze" again while another narrator narrates. Continue "freezing" and "melting" until all the scenes you have chosen have been created.

Give-One-Get-One   To jump-start the thinking, have an essential question displayed on the whiteboard. Challenge students to think and write a brainstorming list in response to the essential question. Display the Give-One-Get-One directions and give each student a Give-One-Get-One handout (see appendix B for a reproducible). Challenge them to decide on three favorite ideas and write them in each of the three boxes in the first row. Students then circulate through the room giving and getting ideas from each other. Time them for about five minutes, and when the time is up, prompt them to be thinking in their heads what idea on their handout can they connect with the most. Students return to their small groups and share their connections.

Young students can draw during the brainstorming component. They will not need the handout. Instead, they will use their drawing. Have students circle their favorite three connections to the prompt and move around the room to share. They can add to their drawings as they share with each other.

WHAT DOES IT TAKE TO BE A METACOGNITIVE LEARNER?

Metacognitive learners monitor their own comprehension, conscious not only of the meaning they are making but also of the adequacy of the processes they are employing to construct that meaning (Costa & Kallick 2009, 118).

Metacognition refers to the ability to recognize and manage what you are thinking, to search for meaning, and to process for understanding.

When being metacognitive, you are actively carrying on that inner conversation and examining your ability to process and progress cognitively. You have an inner dialogue as you learn, are aware of it, and understand the value of it. Equally important, you pay particular attention to when that inner conversation begins to wane, and you find ways to get your thinking back on track.

Students who are metacognitive actively monitor both their thinking process and their progress as they navigate cognitively.

WHAT IS *PROCESS* MONITORING?

According to Marzano, when students are process monitoring, they are paying attention to what their minds are thinking in the midst of learning (Marzano 2001, 49). Marzano and Kendall (2008) use phrases such as "evaluate, determine how well, and determine how effectively" when discussing process monitoring (Marzano & Kendall 2008, 122). If the plan generated breaks down, process monitoring asks for a new or revised plan.

A person who is metacognitive monitors the *process* of thinking in three ways:

1. Metacognitive dialogue
2. Strategic thinking
3. Questioning

The Metacognitive Dialogue

The metacognitive dialogue simply means listening to your own mind. Students who are metacognitve pay attention to their thinking as they learn. They explore the thought process that goes into learning and are aware of what goes on in their minds as they learn. They monitor their thinking before, during, and after learning.

Metacognitive students have an inner conversation throughout the learning, and they pay attention to if and when that dialogue stops. Someone who is metacognitive recognizes the impact that inner voice has on learning.

What matters most is that the metacognitive dialogue is happening. It is not really about finding answers as much as it is about knowing what those answers mean to the learning. It is becoming more aware of the cognitive processes that produced the answers. Just getting the answer is not what is most important. The next time the answer will be different. What matters is the student's understanding of the process used to arrive at the answer so that the process can be refined, altered, or repeated for later problems (Costa & Kallick 2009, 96). Ideally, then, students learn to use this metacognitive dialogue habitually, and it becomes automatic.

How to Improve Your Students'
Metacognitive Dialogue: The Think Aloud

Modeling a think aloud is an important tool in fostering metacognition. It is the perfect venue for giving voice to your inner processing skills. Students appreciate hearing what goes on in your mind as you think. Think alouds make thinking public. They make visible the many complex habits that help us understand. Those habits might include questions, connections to personal experiences and past learning, visualizations, and predictions.

When students stop long enough to listen to their minds at work, they become more aware of their own thinking and give language to it. The think aloud strategy helps students understand how the mind constructs meaning when learning, as well as how it thinks through difficult spots (Costa & Kallick 2009, 123). Another advantage of the think aloud is that it exposes all students to good thinking. There is great power in opening up how you, the teacher, process cognitively.

Many students don't know the teacher uses the same critical thinking habits they are being asked to use. They simply think the teacher is smarter. The benefits of this are amazing. It levels the playing field for those students who never knew "the smart kids" actually do something cognitively in order to process effectively. When students are taught *how* to think rather than *what* to think, it cultivates lifelong learning.

Two of Our Favorite Ideas for Empowering Students to Pay Attention to Their Metacognitive Dialogue

Partner Think Alouds   When a student is encouraged to share his or her thinking with a student who is confused, several things happen. First, the student sharing the thinking gains a deeper understanding of how he or she arrived at that understanding. Second, the student listening gains insight into the "how" of comprehension. And last, but certainly not least, students develop a community of learners, who together are involved in making sense of the learning.

When one student who "gets it" processes his or her thinking with a partner, the academic playing field is officially leveled. It forces the quick processor to slow down and own his or her thinking, and it allows a slower processor the time to engage in the learning in a safe environment. Have students track their thinking process visually. A visual serves as a diagnostic cognitive map of student thinking, which is beneficial for all students in recognizing their ability to be metacognitive.

Exploring Metacognition (Thinking about My Thinking): Double-Entry Reader Response Journal   Students use this advance organizer to hold their thinking as they actively read. It is an important scaffold for students to become more independent and automatic in their metacognitive dialogue. (See appendix B for a template and student handout.)

Students need to set a purpose for reading and question the text as they read to arrive at the connections that are essential for independent readers. (Created and shared by Stephanie Pierce)

Strategic Thinking

Strategic thinking takes complex issues and long-term objectives, which can be very difficult to address, and breaks them down into manageable sizes. Anything becomes simpler when it has a plan (Maxwell 2009, 50).

Strategic thinking is the process of weighing every decision and action in light of current and future circumstances, the direction you want to go in, and the results you want to achieve. It is not about "staying under the radar." It is more about purposefully pushing the envelope in order to make things happen.

So, yes, the ability to think strategically is essential for students to learn in order to succeed in school and in the future. The question is, How can we hone our strategic thinking skills in a way that will positively impact our lives and the lives of our students?

Martin Haworth, from Improvement and Innovation.com, proposes nine essential skills all strategic thinkers possess:

1. *Strategic thinkers have a vision.* Strategic thinkers are purposeful in their planning. They process metacognitively with a vision in mind. They are in tune with their inner thoughts and use them to create that vision. This form of supportive thinking and seeing the future, creates a way of thinking and evolving strategy that is focused and yet broad.
2. *Strategic thinkers are not hasty.* Strategic thinkers linger with and rethink ideas. They are careful thinkers. They understand that they are shaping, coaxing, and fine-tuning their futures by what they think and act on today.
3. *Strategic thinkers absorb and notice.* They are aware of their metacognitive dialogue and use it to their advantage. They pay attention to their own minds and notice when they are getting off track. Great

strategic thinkers take all of this in. It may be an "aha" moment or a subtle connection, but they appreciate and validate it as learning.

4. *Strategic thinkers review often.* The best strategic thinkers monitor their thinking all the time. They repair when necessary and check that their thinking has been validated.

5. *Strategic thinkers learn from experience.* Strategic thinkers use past practice to guide future decisions. They use their experiences, good and bad, to learn.

6. *Strategic thinkers collaborate.* By utilizing more than just their own brain, those great at strategic thinking bounce ideas off others.

7. *Strategic thinkers are realistic visionaries.* Although they are thinking divergently, key strategic thinkers have a sense of realism and honesty about what is achievable in the longer term. They under-promise and overdeliver.

8. *Strategic thinkers have clear milestones.* Strategic thinkers create checks in their thinking—to review progress, to revisit, rethink, and revise thinking. They use these milestones to synthesize and evaluate their progress thus far.

9. *Strategic thinkers are nonjudgmental.* Strategic thinkers do not pass judgment. They appreciate diversity and see it as a strength. (Haworth 2011)

Two of Our Favorite Ideas for Empowering Students to Become Strategic Thinkers

Take Advantage of the Teachable Moments In your classroom, post the above nine essential skills all strategic thinkers possess for all to see. (For younger students, you might want to make the language more "younger kid–friendly.") Now pay close attention to your students. Whenever you see or hear the class, a small group, or an individual effectively use one of the skills, recognize and celebrate it. On the flip side, whenever you notice a missed opportunity, use this as a teaching lesson. Stop the class at some point and use it as a teachable moment. How could they have been more strategic? What might have been the results if they were more strategic? Be careful if you notice an individual student not acting so strategically. Make sure you talk to that student in private. You can also prime the pump by prompting students before they make a decision, suggesting how a strategic thinker would behave in such an instance. Taking advantage of teachable moments can result in some very powerful life lessons. When students are most vulnerable, they are also most open to learning.

Mindful Practice Sessions   Part of being a strategic thinker is having the ability to pay attention to your inner voice, especially when faced with tough decisions. Is it attuned to learning and growing? Challenge your students to do some internal work in order to develop a sense of competence, self-reliance, responsibility, respect, and consequence thinking. Use real challenges in the classroom as a venue for discussion, practice, and role playing. We must take the time to teach the habit of thinking of all possible outcomes, good and bad, before acting. With each decision, are they prepared to accept the possible consequences, now and in the long run?

Questioning to Monitor Our Process

Questions are the driving force when processing. Have I seen this before? Why does this matter? How could it affect me? What is different about what I am learning now? We are in the midst of learning when we question. And when the questions stop, so does learning. Knowing the impact that questioning has on learning is empowering because it is quite simple: metacognitive processing is driven by questions.

If you want to make sense of anything, you have to make sense of it yourself, and that often begins with a question. Asking questions, in any learning, is a signal that you are constructing meaning. Proficient learners ask questions to clarify meaning, connect prior and new information, set a purpose, speculate about text yet to be read, show skepticism, locate a specific answer, and continue to wonder whether or not their questions can be answered (Harvey & Goudvis 2007, 109). If you ask questions as you learn, you are awake. You are thinking.

Teacher-Generated Questions

As teachers, we need to become less concerned with right answers and more concerned with good questions (Allen 2000, 93). Preplanned focused questions preserve the heart of the lesson and empower the students to reach the intended purpose. Higher-level or essential questions will scaffold students to deeper meaning. (See sample questions for monitoring metacognitive process and progress in appendix B.)

Student-Generated Questions

Although many of our students become relatively proficient at answering teacher-generated questions, they sometimes forget the most important questions—their own. When students have questions, they are less likely to abandon the learning (Harvey & Goudvis 2007, 82). Therefore, it only makes sense to nudge our students strongly toward a habit of mind of asking questions.

Two of Our Favorite Ideas for Empowering Students to Use Metacognitive Questioning to Monitor Their Thinking Processes

ReQuest Depending upon the age of the students and your instructional purpose, students either silently read or listen to a portion of text. Include places to pause and reflect on the selection. Partners prepare and ask each other questions about the portion of the text they read or heard. Then the students change roles for the next section of the text. They take turns back and forth, alternating between questioning and responding. As the ReQuest process continues, students learn to imitate good questioning behavior. You may want to use the Question-Answer Relationships (QAR) handout with older students and Thick and Thin questions with younger ones to challenge students to generate a some higher level questions. (See appendix B for sample QAR and Thick and Thin handouts.)

Before, During, and After (BDA) Learning/Reading Question Prompts Students use the BDA Question Prompts advance organizer to encourage and facilitate critical thinking before, during, and after the learning/reading. Of course, the objective is for students to question automatically and naturally, so it is a good idea to remove this scaffold when you notice students consistently questioning to understand. Teachers can use this as well to preplan their high-level questions. (See appendix B for BDA Question Prompts.)

WHAT IS *PROGRESS* MONITORING?

Failing at something is difficult, but failing at something and not knowing what went wrong and where it started to go wrong can be overwhelming. As teachers, we are familiar with process monitoring through the extensive research on comprehension strategy instruction. However, monitoring student progress is sometimes overlooked. It depends upon the individual teacher how much students are taught how to evaluate their own progress. And too often assessments are simply returned with checks and Xs without any explanation as to the mistakes that occurred. How can students learn from this? Unfortunately, then students often repeat the same errors without even knowing it. What happens? The mistakes are repeated, and the cycle continues downward.

Metacognition includes thinking through one's cognitive progression to understanding. Students with good metacognitive skills see the importance of progress monitoring and are armed with the tools to do so. They know what it means to understand, and they are mindful when the progress of that understanding breaks down.

Identifying errors and recognizing what must be done to correct them are critical tools for students to use when analyzing their progress. Monitoring progress is necessary for students to reach success both in and out of school. Our goal is to ultimately have students welcome errors as a healthy part of the learning process.

Identifying and Analyzing Errors

Identifying and analyzing errors is a way of determining how serious an error might be by recognizing, recording, and classifying mistakes. The purposes of error analysis are to (1) identify the patterns of errors or mistakes that students make in their work, (2) understand why students make the errors, and (3) provide targeted instruction to correct the errors (Cohen & Spenciner 2010).

Error analysis empowers students to recognize what they are doing wrong and how to correct it. When conducting an error analysis, the teacher checks the student's mistakes and categorizes the errors (Cohen &

Spenciner 2010, 35). Studies have shown that students benefit more from learning about what they did wrong than what they did right. Additionally, for students to improve their future performance, they need to know why something is wrong. Posamentier and Jaye assert that when students understand why something is wrong, they are more likely to learn appropriate strategies to eliminate their errors (Posamentier & Jaye 2006, 83). The teacher is the facilitator of learning, who asks probing questions and helps students uncover any misunderstandings.

How to Make the Most out of Error Analysis

1. Use student mistakes as opportunities for learning. Deeper understanding comes from recognizing and analyzing errors.
2. Anticipate student misconceptions and common errors in advance of a lesson and have prepared questions/scripts front-loaded for addressing those issues.
3. View flawed solutions as partially correct solutions with underlying logic. Model and think aloud through the correct aspects of a flawed solution.
4. Error analysis engages students as members of a learning community. When class discussion involves collaborative analysis and revision of flawed solutions, there are often opportunities for students to think about underlying concepts.
5. Intellectual risk taking is promoted because mistakes are viewed as opportunities for learning (National Council of Teachers of Mathematics 2011, 438–39).

Two of Our Favorite Ideas for Empowering Students to Identify and Analyze Errors

Checking for Accuracy   As teachers, we have all felt bewildered by students handing in careless work and being satisfied with it. We repeatedly challenge our students to check their work—all the while watching them quickly eyeball it as they walk toward us to hand it in. What's a teacher to do? The answer is simple: teach students to value accuracy. The task, however, takes time and effort.

Here are some great ways to help students value accuracy and strive for exemplary work:

- Return tests without all the checks and Xs. Instead, on each page, write something like, "You have two common mistakes on the concept of _____ on this page. Find them and tell me what you did wrong and how you will fix it."
- When you introduce a project, provide exemplary work for students to see.
- Create rubrics for all performance assessments, and provide ample time before, during, and after the project to ask questions, self-monitor progress, do peer reviews, and make improvements.
- Brainstorm and write the criteria for projects along with the students. Begin by asking the students what they think an exemplary project would need to include.
- Use an answer key as a tool—include answer keys with all the work included and allow students to use them to discover their inaccuracies and find the reasons for them.
- Do a think aloud on how you check over your work—what it looks like and sounds like to check for accuracy. Have students write down what they notice you doing to check for accuracy. Make a poster and use it as a resource.
- Provide samples of varying levels of work; have students grade them using your rubric and justify their grading.
- Give corrections for credit—make sure students include what went wrong and how they fixed it.
- Have career professionals come in and share how important it is to do a job right the first time.
- Model the importance of checking for accuracy in your teaching. Include questions like these:
  ○ How could we verify or test that?
  ○ How could we find out if that is true?
  ○ How reliable is my source?
  ○ How do I know if this is fact or just an opinion?
- Catch students before they fail:
  ○ Provide study sessions before an assessment.
  ○ Include small group instruction as part of daily practice.

○ Offer plenty of time to reflect on progress.
○ Use metacognitive dialogue journals, in which students reflect on their thinking process and progress along with you.
○ Create additional, alternative opportunities for students to provide evidence that they understand the concepts.

Grade Defense We first heard about this idea from Lee Newman, a national educational consultant. Grade defense empowers students to appreciate checking for accuracy not only as important, but as their responsibility. (See an example of grade defense in mathematics in appendix B.)

We follow the grade defense procedure below, but it is easy to tweak to better suit any purpose, with any grade level:

- Share your objectives and show exemplary examples of the project.
- Have students brainstorm evaluation criteria in small groups. Come to a class consensus on criteria that would best represent the learning objectives.
- Create a rubric that chunks the project into two phases. The first phase includes a self-assessment piece. Make sure this is strategically placed at a midway point or before students go to final draft. The second phase is your assessment of the final draft and presentation of the project and/or writing piece.
- Make and post an appointment calendar and have students sign up for a grade defense meeting with you.
- Give clear directives as to what part of the project is to be completed before they can meet with you and what they are expected to bring to the meeting. Include the student in deciding what portion of the project will be reviewed. Include a self-assessment piece on the first component of the project. They should bring the self-assessment with them when meeting with you and should be prepared to share their thoughts and reflections thus far.
- The student should lead the meeting, defending the project against the evaluation criteria in the rubric. You are listening to their defense as the student shows you what he or she has done so far, how the student feels he or she is doing, and how the student plans to finish the project.

- If you agree, you finalize the grade for that part and the student can move on to the final part of the project or begin the final draft. If you don't agree, you both discuss points for improvement. The student has the opportunity to make the necessary changes and meet again.
- After the student has successfully defended his or her grade thus far, the student receives full credit for that part of the project and has approval to continue to final draft.

To be honest, our first impression was, "Yea, sure, who has all that time?" But the meetings are quite short and don't interfere with teaching because we held them when students were working in small groups or independently. The benefits were huge! Students were more engaged, careful, and excited about the work they were completing.

LEARNING GOALS

Elbert Hubbard said, "Many people fail in life, not for the lack of ability or even courage but simply because they have never organized their energies around a goal." President Obama agrees with this statement so much that he has included the idea of goal setting as part of a national initiative.

The president is challenging us as a nation to become more goal oriented. As part of his national proposal for healthy living, he includes four important steps to creating achievable goals:

1. *Be realistic.* Goals should be challenging and rigorous, but attainable. An unreachable goal will only be discouraging.
2. *Think short-term.* Goals must be meaningful and reachable in the near future.
3. *Write it down.* Kids and adults alike benefit from writing out their goals and putting them where they can see them every day.
4. *Keep it simple.* Goals should be straightforward. ("Get Motivated" [n.d.])

Instruction that promotes metacognition asks students to think about their learning goals, select appropriate strategies for pursing those goals, and reflect on the effectiveness of their chosen approach (Jackson 2011b,

16). A metacognitive approach to instruction can help students learn to take control of their learning by defining learning goals and monitoring their progress in achieving them (Wiggins & McTighe 2005, 316).

Directly teaching students how to effectively and realistically plan is an important instructional strategy, especially for those students who often begin a task but do not finish (Marzano & Kendall 2008, 117). Students need to be taught specific strategies for goal setting. Part of the instruction should focus on how to redirect and revise goals whenever a problem arises.

The Northwest Educational Technology Consortium (NETC), based on the landmark work of Marzano, Pickering, and Pollock (2001), offers suggestions for helping students create learning goals:

- Student ownership makes a difference. Ask students to create their own goals. Help them personalize and refine their own set of goals by sharing examples, modeling the process, or creating strategies for documenting and completion. Model how you reflect on your progress and what you do when a problem arises.
- It is the students themselves who need to consciously work out a strategy for success. Provide practice and modeling on how to do this effectively.
- Students might visualize the accomplished goal to help them strategize how to carry out the task.
- Allow students time to adopt goals. Allow sufficient time to revisit and revise goals.
- Use advance organizers to introduce goals. Advance organizers can help students prepare for, focus on, and personalize goals.
- Help students understand different kinds of goals. There are short-term and long-term goals. In classrooms with different instructional practices, often in middle and high school, setting and meeting objectives may need to take many forms. Provide students practice in setting personal goals and meeting them in different contexts.
- Focus goals on understanding. Ensure that goals are less about accomplishing tasks and more focused on understanding and applying concepts. School communities can support goal setting with agreed upon consistent structure across the content areas.

- Come back to the goals often, so that they are aware of their own learning and progress. Challenge students to question their progress. How's it working for them? Is what they are currently doing helping or hurting them in achieving their goal? ("Focus on Effectiveness" [n.d.])

Two of Our Favorite Ideas for Empowering Students to Create and Evaluate Learning Goals

Make, Revisit, Rethink, and Revise Working Goals Whenever students are working on long-term projects, begin the work session by challenging them to make short-term working goals. Students begin by reviewing the rubric, the expectations, the due date, and what they have accomplished so far. Then, after distilling all this, students decide on a goal to accomplish before the end of the scheduled work time. To build in accountability, require students to write down their goal for the day and share it with a partner.

Halfway through the work time, students revisit that goal. How are they doing so far? Do they need to revise the goal a bit to be more realistic? Are they using their time wisely? If not, why not and what can they do to get back on track? Have students reflect on their ability to stay focused, work hard, and achieve their goal again at the end of work time. Making this a regular part of long-term projects teaches students how to manage their way through them successfully.

Tracking Your Progress to Standardized Testing This idea comes from Audra Ritter, a special education teacher at Coatesville Area School District in Pennsylvania. Audra was teaching a self-contained eighth-grade mathematics class at the time. She began the year using a diagnostic assessment to see where her students were mathematically. She used the scores as a starting point. Audra then created a timeline for each student and a little figure that represented each of them. She provided the score each student would need to get in order to be considered proficient in mathematics. She continued to assess her students along the way, providing them the feedback they needed to keep track of their progress. With every score they received, they moved their figure closer to the target goal. And guess what? Every one of her students scored proficient that year.

HOW CAN I BECOME A MORE METACOGNITIVE TEACHER?

The Backwards Design Model for Instructional Planning

In the best-selling book *The 7 Habits of Highly Effective People*, Stephen Covey conveys that effective people plan with the end in mind (Covey 2004). This idea stands for teaching as well. As teachers, planning with the end in mind is being metacognitive in design of instruction.

Backwards design is a way of thinking more purposefully and carefully about the nature of any design that has understanding as the goal (Wiggins & McTighe 2005, 7). The backwards design model centers on the idea that the design process should begin with identifying the desired results and then work backwards to develop instruction. The object of backwards design is to make understanding more likely by design rather than by luck, with deliberate and explicit instruction (Wiggins & McTighe 2005, 17).

Backwards design is no different than using Google Maps. Before your directions are planned out, you must first plug in a beginning point and an ending destination. Highly effective metacognitive instruction is the same way. You begin where your students are, you plan a purposeful destination, and you bring those students along for the journey. Grant Wiggins and Jay McTighe (2005) have masterfully set out for us what it takes to become more metacognitive and purposeful in our instructional design. Here are the three stages of backwards design:

Stage 1: Identify desired goals, outcomes, and essential understandings. What do you want students to walk away with as a result of your lesson/ unit? What should students understand as a result of the activities or the content covered? Unpack the lesson objective in a way that entices and engages students. Rewriting standards as essential questions provides easier access to the learning.

- *The essential question.* Determine the purpose of the lesson. From that, create an open-ended, engaging question that is in kid-friendly language. Have it posted to ignite student thinking right away. Ask students to think, write, and discuss their responses. (For little ones, they can sketch or just think in their heads, then share with a partner.)

  Revisit the question again halfway through the lesson. Challenge students to rethink and revise their original answers. Have them share their responses with a different partner and add anything new to their thinking if desired.

Have students revisit the essential question a final time when you debrief the lesson. This time, use their new knowledge to add and revise their original responses. Allow time for quiet conversation. (See sample from a science lesson in appendix B.)

Stage 2: Determine what constitutes acceptable evidence of competency in the outcomes and results. How will you know if they got there? What would be evidence that learners are en route to the desired abilities and insights?

- *"Have a scrapbook of evidence as opposed to a single snapshot"* (Wiggins & McTighe 2005, 188). Assessments come in many forms: open-ended question prompts, self-assessments, choral responses, menus, contracts, centers, problem-based scenarios, entrance and exit tickets, projects, quizzes, tests, formative assessments, and so on. Formative assessments help students monitor their own understanding. They are ongoing assessments used as part of the instructional process. First, the teacher must know what it is that the students need to know to demonstrate deep understanding and mastery of the concept.

Stage 3: Plan instructional strategies and learning experiences that carry students to the intended learning goal. What engaging and effective instructional practices will bring them to this understanding? How then should activities and resources be chosen and used to ensure that the learning goals are met and the most appropriate evidence produced? (Wiggins & McTighe 2005).

Providing Meaningful Feedback

The single most powerful modification in instruction to enhance achievement is to provide meaningful feedback (Hattie, Biggs, & Purdie 1996, 9). Meaningful feedback allows students to consider their progress, understand what they know and can do, be confident in their learning, and discover what they must still learn. Ultimately, we want students to analyze, evaluate, and reflect on their own progress (Posamentier & Jaye 2006, 106).

Feedback that is specific and consistent has a strong effect on student success. Feedback must be specific to the topic, diagnostic as well as prescriptive, and given often. Teacher feedback should be presented in a way that is supportive and encourages students to take action, apply it, and see improvement.

Sometimes teachers believe they should display only perfect student work—but really, what is perfect work? Instead, focus more on the progress each student is making. Include feedback that is growth oriented. Of course, begin with a positive, but make sure the positive comment provides detail as to what is so great about it. Then, students know what they are doing well. A simple "Excellent work" will not offer the feedback students need. How about something like, "Excellent work. I love the way you showed all your steps with such clarity. It really made it easy to follow!"

Next try to include a growth point. We all have them, and students need to know where they need to go to see progress. This instills a growth mindset. The truth is we are all a work in progress. Some call this strategy for giving feedback, "Star, Wish, Star" which basically means begin with a positive that is meaningful, include a wish that you would like to see in the future, and end with another positive. Another very productive way to give feedback is the "Stars and Stairs" method. You draw a star and give your positive but detailed feedback. Then draw a simple sketch of stairs and give your point of growth.

Marzano, Pickering, and Pollock have created the following generalizations to guide teachers in the use of meaningful feedback (Marzano, Pickering, & Pollock 2001, 96–99):

1. *Feedback should be "corrective" in nature.* In other words, the best feedback involves an explanation as to what is accurate and what is inaccurate.
2. *Feedback should be timely.* In general, the more delay in giving feedback, the less improvement there is in achievement.
3. *Feedback should be specific to a criterion.* For feedback to be most useful, it should reference a specific level of skill or knowledge. Generally, the more specific feedback is the better.

4. *Students can effectively provide some of their own feedback.* Students should simply keep track of their performance as learning occurs. Self-evaluation is strongly advocated.

When students become aware of what's going on inside their heads, they recognize the potential of metacognition. As teachers, there is no better gift than providing students with the capacity to become tuned in to the power of their own thinking.

LIFELONG LEARNERS ARE METACOGNITIVE

And once I had a teacher who understood: he brought with him the beauty of the subject. He made me create it for myself. He gave me nothing, and it was more than any other teacher has ever dared to give me.

—L. Cochran, *Journal of Mathematical Behavior*, 1991

Lifelong learners acquire a keen awareness of their minds at work. They can identify and describe understanding and are able to cultivate the processes of metacognition to direct their own cognitive and social learning.

Lifelong Learners Are Divergent Thinkers

We need people who can read and write. But what we really need is people who can not only read the instructions but change them. They need to be able to think outside the lines.

—Richard Gurin, CEO and
president of Binney & Smith Crayola Products

WHAT IS DIVERGENT THINKING?

The Merriam-Webster definition of *divergent thinking* is "creative thinking that may follow many lines of thought and tends to generate new and original solutions to problems." It is the capacity to act and think flexibly and creatively with what one knows.

Divergent thinking is an essential capacity for creativity to occur. It is not quite the same thing as creativity. Creativity is the process of having original ideas that have value. Divergent thinking is the ability to see lots of possible answers to a question and lots of possible ways of interpreting a question (McKeown 2011).

Divergent thinkers are unafraid to take risks. They appreciate a good problem, exploring options and creating backup plans that provide alternative solutions. Divergent thinkers often find solutions when no one else can. They don't let the ideas that *don't* work prevent them from coming up with more ideas that *do* work (Maxwell 2009, 27).

WHY IS DIVERGENT THINKING IMPORTANT
TO BECOMING A LIFELONG LEARNER?

Divergent thinkers know they must repeatedly break out of the "box" of their own history and personal limitations in order to experience creative breakthroughs (Keene 2008, 208). Popular thinking said the earth was the center of the universe; yet Copernicus studied the stars and planets and proved mathematically that the earth and other planets in our solar system revolved around the sun.

If we are to succeed in a constantly changing world, we must acknowledge, value, and cultivate divergent thinking. It is time to dismiss the idea that knowledge can simply be transferred from one source to another. The demands of this world will not allow it. The challenge of the twenty-first century is to find creative solutions to multidimensional problems crossing many boundaries such as conflict, poverty, ignorance, racial and gender inequity, unemployment, hunger, and apathy.

To achieve this goal, our students need to know how to

- Generate new ideas
- Value and use questioning to shape new understandings
- Problem solve creatively
- Be flexible
- Embrace change
- Access information from a wide array of resources, gain meaning from it, and apply it in real-life situations
- Appreciate different perspectives
- Assimilate learning in new ways

WHAT COGNITIVE PROCESSES
FOSTER DIVERGENT THINKING?

1. Visualizing

Psychologists believe in the dual-coding model of information storage (Pavio 1990). This theory proposes that knowledge is stored in two forms: a linguistic form and a nonlinguistic or image form. Robert Marzano confirms that the more we employ both systems of representation, linguistic and nonlinguistic, the better we are at reasoning and recalling information (Marzano 2007, 73).

Visualizing has the power to expand on students' knowledge base. Explicitly engaging them in the creation of representations stimulates and increases activity in the brain, promoting dual confirmation of the learning.

When we teach through representations, we challenge students to generate alternative strategies for solving problems, a significant ingredient in divergent thinking. We agree with Costa and Kallick when they say, "It is better to teach three ways to solve one problem than it is to teach one way to solve three problems" (Costa & Kallick 2009, 38). Visualizing is often the foundation to deep, critical, divergent thinking.

Two of Our Favorite Ideas for Empowering Students to Visualize

Read Alouds   The read aloud holds a hidden power when it comes to teaching visualization, in that, when students are being read to, it forces them to conjure up their own pictures.

Picture books are especially useful in teaching visualizing because many are written using such beautiful descriptive language. We have included an anchor lesson idea on visualization that comes from an outstanding educational consultant, Ann Moorcones. She recommends using the book *Where the River Begins* by Thomas Locker. This lesson was modeled by Ann in many classrooms across the country. It is intended for grades 2–6 but can be adapted for any age group. (See appendix C for Ann's detailed lesson plans.)

- The following are additional children's books recommended by Debbie Miller for teaching visualizing (Miller 2002, 42).
  Close Your Eyes by Jean Marzollo
  Color Me a Rhyme by Jane Yolen
  Creatures of Earth, Sea, and Sky by Georgia Heard
  Footprints and Shadows by Anne Westcott Dodd
  Goodnight to Annie by Eve Merriam
  Greyling by Jane Yolen
  I Am the Ocean by Suzanna Marshak
  The Napping House by Audrey Wood

Night in the Country by Cynthia Rylant
Night Sounds, Morning Colors by Rosemary Wells
Putting the World to Sleep by Shelley Moore Thomas
Quiet, Please by Eve Merriam
The Salamander Room by Anne Mazer
Say Something by Mary Stoltz
What Does the Rain Play? by Nancy White Carlstrom
When I'm Sleepy by Jane R. Howard
Wild, Wild Sunflower Child by Nancy White Carlstrom
The Zoo at Night by Martha Robinson

Using Nonlinguistic Representations with Informational Texts

- T-Notes Plus
  - Ahead of time, have students create the front cover of a blank manila folder like the one in figure 4.1 and cut along the dashed cut lines. Students should be able to fit their notes in the folder.

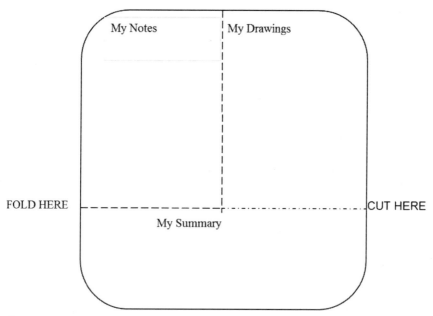

Figure 4.1

○ Students will create a similar setup in their notes. As they either read an excerpt from the text or listen to a lecture, they include the important ideas using words and drawings. Students summarize the learning at the bottom section of the page.

○ Have students fold the front cover back along the vertical center fold line, then up along the horizontal fold line near the bottom, and return the folder to its original flat position.

○ Students slide their notes into the folder for "T-Notes Plus Study Strategy"

1. Cover the written summary and try to mentally summarize what you learned. Check to see if your summary is similar to the one you wrote.

2. Cover the notes and look at your drawings. Do you remember what they stand for?

3. Review the notes section to see if your recall was accurate. Reread the notes to find important details.

4. Add any questions you have on the back of the notes paper.

5. Do this every night as a quick way to review your notes. (Beninghof 2006, 66–67)

- Split Screen
  1. Ahead of time, create a graphic organizer that looks like a TV with a split screen. Title the left screen "Images" and the right screen "Thinking behind My Images."

  2. Select a short piece of text to read aloud. Students will listen and sketch what they consider to be the big ideas on the left screen. Pause periodically so students have time to sketch.

  3. When the reading is finished, students share the images in pairs and are free to add or revise their sketches. Together they write the meaning behind their sketches on the right screen.

  4. Select a piece of text for students to read independently. Students begin with a "before reading" strategy, such as skimming and scanning text features to identify a purpose and theme.

  5. As they read, students respond to the text by sketching on the left screen. They pause periodically to write an explanation of those images. Students continue this until they finish the text.

  6. Small groups compare and contrast split screens. Give students a moment to add or revise the sketches and explanations after sharing.

2. Identifying Similarities and Differences

Robert Marzano considers identifying similarities and differences to be the core of all learning (Marzano 2007, 64). Classifying according to features or characteristics helps students develop a scheme, a way to organize objects and ideas. This approach allows the brain to process new information, recall it, and learn by overlaying a known pattern onto an unknown one while finding similarities and differences.

Analytical thinking helps students chunk information, attaching individual ideas to others in their minds as if they were fitting puzzle pieces together on a tabletop. Teachers can lead students to these discoveries through intentional instruction that builds meaning through effective comparison.

Students benefit by having similarities and differences pointed out to them by the teacher in an explicit manner. Identifying similarities and differences can jumpstart students' thinking about big ideas. And big ideas take big thinking—a fertile ground for cultivating divergent thinking.

Marzano, Pickering, and Pollock recognize comparing and classifying as two highly effective forms of identifying similarities and differences:

- *Comparing*: identifying similarities and differences between or among concepts
- *Classifying*: grouping like things into categories on the basis of their characteristics (Marzano, Pickering, & Pollock 2001, 26)

Two of Our Favorite Ideas for Empowering Students to Identify Similarities and Differences

Instructional Ideas That Promote Classifying and Categorizing
- Affinity Charts
    1. Hand out sticky notes to each person.
    2. Declare a broad topic.
    3. Instruct students to put one word or phrase on each sticky note.
    4. Place the sticky notes on the whiteboard or wall.
    5. All participants must stand and silently move the sticky notes into groups that make sense.
    6. Finally, have the group decide on a title for each grouping.

7. The information gained can be recorded and passed out to each person or team.

- *List-Group-Label.* Either prepare words in advance or have students brainstorm a list of words around a topic. Students use the words and group them into categories that make sense. Then challenge students to create a meaningful title for each category. They should be able to defend the reasoning behind each title. This is a great way to begin a unit of study. Repeat the activity at the end of the unit as a postassessment.

- *Open or Closed Word Sorts.* Classifying can be done as an *open* or *closed* sort. In a closed sort, students organize words into predetermined categories that you develop. In an open sort, students determine the categories. The key to divergent thinking is in being able to explain the reasoning behind each category. Not everyone will have the same groups, but everyone should be able to defend their groups with understanding.

- *Secret Sorts.* Challenge small groups to create categories of words around a topic of study. They should not reveal titles for the categories. Have students visit each secret sort in a gallery walk, trying to identify category choices.

- *Circle the Category.* Ahead of time, prepare titles and words that would fit in each category. Distribute the titles only to certain students and have them stand up and spread out somewhere in the classroom. Hand out a word card to the remaining students. Challenge students to "circle the category" where they feel their word belongs. They should discuss their reasoning in the circle (Forsten, Grant, & Hollas 2002).

- *Double-Dutch Chants.* Start with a word sort, then read aloud an excerpt from *Double Dutch: A Celebration of Jump Rope, Rhyme, and Sisterhood* by Veronica Chambers. Push the divergent thinking by having students develop their own jump rope chants based on their favorite category. Bring in a double-dutch jump rope. The power lies in the physical act of jumping and chanting.

- *Working Word Wall.* Small groups write vocabulary cards with an invented definition and a picture. Create a word wall bulletin board. At different points during a unit, provide opportunities to categorize the concepts and create hierarchies using the words. Have students defend their choices.

- *Bottle Cap Sort.* Ahead of time write either numbers or words on bottle caps. Put them into baggies and give one to each group. Students can do an open or closed sort using the caps. You can also have students compare using a Venn diagram. Provide categories and have students use the caps to compare and contrast. To deepen the thinking, challenge students to place the caps on the Venn diagram according to a mystery comparison. Have groups visit another team's arrangement to see if they can identify the reasoning behind the comparison (Benninghof 2010, 103).

Using Graphic Organizers That Promote Identifying Similarities and Differences   The use of graphic organizers enhances student understanding of content. Have students create and/or use graphic organizers of similarities and differences, classification systems, comparisons, examples and counterexamples, and analogies. Possible suggestions include the following:

- Venn diagrams—two to four-circle comparisons
- Hierarchies
- Matrixes and attribute charts
- Mind maps
- T-charts for examples and nonexamples
- Tree diagrams
- Bubble maps and double bubble maps to link comparisons
- Brace maps—as in March Madness brackets

Questioning

Did you ever spend a morning in a preschool? Little children are naturally curious about everything. Regrettably, what is second nature to our younger students often dissipates as they move into the intermediate grades (Kelly & Clausen-Grace 2007). In fact, by the time students are in fourth grade, their problem-solving skills suffer because of a profound lack of thinking and questioning (Hyde 2006, 17).

Questioning is often thought of as the conduit for divergent thinking. Scientists use questions during the process of discovery all the time. Every invention more than likely began with a question. Albert Einstein attested to this when he said, "I have no special talent: I am only passionately curious."

Two of Our Favorite Ideas for Empowering Students to Use Questioning to Promote Divergent Thinking

Change the Style of Questions Asked   Questions that promote divergent thinking are open-ended, engaging, and thought provoking. They cannot be answered in one or two words. If our desire is for students to think divergently, then good questioning strategies should be at the forefront of our instruction.

Asking and answering questions plays a significant role in developing creativity and divergent thinking. That sense of childhood wonder can be recaptured if students remain curious about learning, and good questioning allow that to happen.

- *Preplan questions that will promote divergent thinking.* Copy the following prompts and keep them on hand when you are teaching. Decide in advance which ones you will include in your lesson to promote deeper, more critical thinking.
  - What makes you say that?
  - How do you know you're right?
  - What's another way of thinking about . . . ?
  - What qualities of a lifelong learner do you see evident here? How do you know?
  - What qualities of a lifelong learner are missing here? How would the result be different if they were present?
  - What are your thoughts on . . . ?
  - Why do you think so?
  - What would you do in this instance? Why?
  - What's a different way to . . . ? What else?
  - What strategy makes the most sense to use in this instance? What makes you say that?
  - What strategy would definitely not work in this situation? What makes you say that?
  - What else would you like to add to . . . ?

- *Questions on sticky notes.* Have students learn to read actively by responding to the text. Provide sticky notes for students to hold their thinking. They should place the sticky notes right in the text. If questions are answered, encourage students to place the question where the answer is found. If there are still unanswered questions, have students save them to discuss with others, either in a small or large group setting.
- *Answer a question with a question.* Don't provide the answers too quickly. Let students wrestle with the learning. Do not solve every problem; help students acquire the tools they need to solve problems on their own.

3. Thinking Metaphorically

Researchers have found that employing the use of analogies and metaphors in instruction has been proven to help boost student achievement from 31 to 46 percentile points (Ross 1987; Stahl & Fairbanks 1986).

Making metaphorical connections stretches student thinking and increases their understanding. In this way, students are taught critical thinking skills that stay with them long after the lesson.

Marzano, Pickering, and Pollock recognize creating metaphors and analogies as two highly effective forms of identifying similarities and differences.

- *Creating metaphors.* Identifying a general or basic pattern in a specific topic and then finding another topic that appears to be quite different but has the same general pattern.
- *Creating analogies.* Identifying relationships between pairs of concepts—in other words, identifying relationships between relationships (Marzano, Pickering, & Pollock 2001, 26).

Creative Ideas That Foster Metaphorical Thinking
- *Creating cartoons, comic strips, or superheroes to illustrate a key concept.* Have students design original cartoons, comic strips, or superheroes to illustrate a key concept taught. For example, students could design a comic book in which the main character is Square, a superhero with all the strengths and powers specific to his nature.

- *Constructing a character homepage or avatar.*
- *Designing advertisements.* Students create an advertisement slogan that describes an important concept, famous historical or scientific person or event, or character. Be creative and thoughtful when writing the advertisement slogan. Proof of research and supporting details must be evident in the slogan. Students can either present it as a TV commercial or create an illustration for a magazine or news journal.
- *Creating "wanted posters."* Students create "wanted posters" that describe an important concept, famous historical or scientific person or event, or character from a story. Wanted posters should include a "mug shot," a description of the "criminal" with connections to the learning included, what they are "wanted" for, any warnings, their aliases, who they associate with, the DOB, last known address, and any identifying marks. Challenge students to use research to defend their choices.
- *Designing an experiment.* Design an experiment around a topic of study. Students will need to write up the experiment in detail, have enough materials for the class to do it, and be able to explain the research behind the experiment. Partner experiments are also useful.
- *Creating a song/rap/jingle.* Create a song, rap, or jingle representing a topic of study. It must have a main theme in both melody and lyrics. The lyrics should convey accurate content information and should be creative and the details should support the main theme. A live performance is required and must be rehearsed well in advance. If you choose, both lyrics and music can be required.
- *Writing a skit, role playing, or acting it out.* Have students demonstrate their learning by acting it out. Students could present in groups or alone. This activity is fun and makes a visual and physical frame of reference.
- *Writing a poem.* Students write poems around a topic of study. They must include supporting details, accurate information, and evidence of the learning. They should communicate the learning in a creative way.
- *Designing a field trip.* Engage students in designing a school or local community field trip for students in a lower grade. The students can develop an observation or record sheet for the younger students to complete as they engage in the field trip. By thinking about what the

younger students will learn from the experience, the older students are reinforcing their own concepts and understanding in a critical way (Tate 2009, 20).

- *Packing a suitcase.* Challenge students to pack an imaginary suitcase for a fictional character or a famous person. Make sure they can defend their choices with supporting details and accurate information. Ask students to choose a destination for the person and explain why they chose it. Would the character be alone? Why or why not? Would they need to bring any of the qualities of a lifelong learner? Which ones? Why? Would they deliberately leave one of the qualities out of the suitcase? Why?

WHAT DOES IT TAKE TO BE A DIVERGENT THINKER?

Gone are the days when we can go around mentally in neutral. Our society craves innovative thinkers, those who are on the cutting edge of discovery and are constantly pushing to improve. In order to be competitive in the twenty-first century, we must think and act outside the box.

Divergent thinkers can think on their feet. Let's consider just one example, the TV show *Top Chef.* Every episode includes a "Quick-Fire Challenge," in which each chef is given a single, usually very weird ingredient to build a meal around—all in one hour. How do they get through it? Divergent thinking. No one is provided a recipe or even a helpful hint. Yet they all create something in the hour. These chefs thrive in the uncertainty of the moment. And what do they create? Pigskin ravioli, hot and sour eggplants, flash-fried rattlesnake with a brown butter sauce. It is the handiwork of true creativity. Divergent thinkers can stand the heat enough to stay in the kitchen and flourish.

Being Comfortable in Ambiguity

"Only by wrestling with the conditions of the problem at hand, seeking and finding his own way out, does he think" (Dewey 1933, 159). These words show that John Dewey realized the importance of divergent thinking. Divergent thinkers don't strive for certainty. They embrace ambiguity as their canvas for growth and learning.

John Maxwell, in his book *How Successful People Think*, believes that how we handle uncertainty will often reveal a lot about us as people. He explains that divergent thinkers see all kinds of inconsistencies and gaps in life, and they often take delight in exploring those gaps—or in using their intelligence to fill them in (Maxwell 2009, 25).

We, as teachers, need to provide conditions where solutions are not immediately evident, where students are forced to find order in what appears to be chaotic. Cris Tovanni supports the idea that students depend on opportunities to wrestle with the learning when she states, "Meaning does not arrive, it must be constructed" (Tovanni 2004, 104).

For divergent thinking to flourish, students must be left to sort through confusion to gain clarity. Simply "telling" does not work. Learning is a constructive process. Periods of disequilibrium brought on by new ideas is where divergent thinking comes alive.

Students can only truly understand what they have constructed themselves. How can teachers promote a constructivist approach to learning?

True learning takes place only when students engage with the information deeply enough to merge that content into their personal views and understandings of how the world works.

We offer three options for empowering students to thrive in the uncertainty of life and construct meaning from it.

- *Provide guided inquiry and discovery*. When students learn by discovery, they are much more likely to understand, remember, and apply their learning to other situations (Allen 2000, 123). Guided inquiry requires students to work together to solve problems, defend solutions, and evaluate decisions as opposed to the teacher giving students all the information they need up front.

  Discovery learning uses innate curiosity to the student's advantage. The teacher's job in discovery learning is not to impart knowledge but, instead, to facilitate students' progress along the path of discovering knowledge themselves.
- *Offer problem-based learning experiences*. Problem-based learned began in the 1950s as an advancement to reform medical school education. It received such success that problem-based learning spread out to classrooms everywhere. Teachers provide a natural setting for divergent thinking when initiating a problem for students to solve.

Teaching from a problem-based learning framework has the following advantages:

° It is student-centered.
° Students find it more enjoyable and satisfying.
° It encourages greater understanding.
° It furthers divergent thinking.
° Students with problem-based learning experience rate their abilities higher.
° Problem-based learning develops lifelong learning skills. (Pawson et al. 2006)

- *Generating and testing a hypothesis.* Hypothesizing is considered a high-yield activity during and after a learning experience because it engages students in analyzing, applying, and reassessing their knowledge (Marzano 2003, 80). Students employ higher order thinking skills when generating ideas, and divergent thinking comes into play whenever they are expected to test out those ideas. This is fertile ground for invention and new discoveries to flourish.

THINKING IN NOVEL WAYS

To diverge means to expand options, to break out. It signifies deviating from the norm to access new ideas. Divergent thinking is an essential quality of creativity. People who are divergent thinkers are novel thinkers. They do not rely on the ordinary. When making decisions, they "diverge" in all directions, only to discover extraordinary answers. Divergent thinkers create countless alternatives, ideas, and answers to any given situation.

Divergent thinkers are able to do something new, think something that has never been thought before. They try new things in new ways (Maxwell 2009, 89). Divergent thinkers can look at what appears to be a lost cause and see possibilities. They are not intimidated by roadblocks. To divergent thinkers, detours are not an option. They imagine several paths to a solution and move toward making them work.

Divergent thinkers are the backbone of innovation in our economy. Think of Larry Page and Sergey Brinn (Google), Steven Jobs (Apple), and Mark Zuckerberg (Facebook)—all masters of divergent thinking. They each brought a different approach to thinking, created new standards, and revolutionized the way people use information to communicate and learn.

As a matter of fact, history is full of great divergent thinkers.

Two of Our Favorite Ideas for Empowering Students to Think in Novel Ways

Brainstorming Alex Osborn coined the technique in 1953 in his book *Applied Imagination*. He suggested that businesses could double their creative productivity with brainstorming (Osborn 1953). Brainstorming is used in all areas of life. It is a highly successful way to generate lots of ideas on a specific topic, and then determine which idea is the best option. It is the perfect venue for divergent thinking to occur. Ideas flow freely in a brainstorming session, and students are given a variety of ideas to explore.

Here are some general directions for brainstorming:

1. Choose an idea, essential question, or problem to use for the brainstorming topic. It should be open-ended and thought-provoking enough to generate lots of responses.
2. Decide if the brainstorming will be done independently to stimulate research or writing ideas, in small groups for problem-solving and activating background knowledge, or whole group for building interest.
3. Introduce the following rules for brainstorming:
   - Present the brainstorming topic.
   - Decide whether students will brainstorm independently, in small groups, or with the whole class.
   - Set a time and adhere to it.
   - Students list as many ideas as possible within that time.
   - All ideas are listed; there is no judgment or evaluation in a brainstorming session.
4. Students can process the list several ways. They can evaluate each idea and decide on their favorite two or three ideas generated. Students may also prioritize the top five ideas. If students need to decide on one idea from the top five chosen, they can use a very popular method that's called "Spend-a-dot."

Spend-a-dot is a great way for groups to prioritize ideas generated in brainstorming. Give each person three dots to spend. They decide how to use them. Three dots can be placed on what they consider to be the most important idea, or they can be spread out between two or three ideas. When everyone places their dots, the idea with the most dots takes top priority. Spend-a-dot is especially effective in large group settings such as professional development situations.

Here are some basic rules to follow when facilitating a brainstorming session in the classroom:

1. There are no wrong answers.
2. Try to get as many ideas as possible.
3. Record all ideas.
4. Do not express your evaluation on any idea. (Watson n.d.)

Freewriting Freewriting is a great technique to begin almost any creative endeavor. It is a way of tapping into our deeper selves (Costa & Kallick 2009, 138).

In his book *Writing with Power*, Elbow proposes the following guidelines on freewriting:

- Write nonstop for a set period of time (the time depends upon your purpose).
- Do not make corrections as you write.
- Keep pen to paper.
- Write whatever comes to mind.
- Do not judge or censor what you are writing.

According to Elbow, freewriting has the following benefits:

- It makes you more comfortable with the act of writing.
- It is nonjudgmental and not threatening.
- It generates many ideas.
- It promotes divergent thinking.
- It encourages creativity.
- It can be a reflective.

- It can help you discover more ideas to write about.
- It can indirectly improve your formal writing.
- It is engaging. (Elbow 1998)

LOOKING AT THINGS FROM DIFFERENT PERSPECTIVES

We enhance the habit of thinking divergently when we alter our perspective and see things from other points of view (Erwin 2010, 100). In effect, John Maxwell contends that one of the most important skills we can develop is the ability to see things from the other person's point of view (Maxwell 2009, 7).

Being able to see things from someone else's perspective is fundamental to becoming a lifelong learner. It means we recognize we don't have all the answers. We understand that we don't have to be right all the time. The benefits of looking at things from different perspectives go far beyond the classroom. It is a vital ingredient to every relationship.

> If there is any one secret of success, it lies in the ability to get the other person's point of view and see things from that person's angle as well as from your own.
>
> —Henry Ford

> I've always felt that a person's intelligence is directly reflected by the number of conflicting points of view he can entertain simultaneously on the same topic.
>
> —Abigail Adams

Need we say more?

Two of Our Favorite Ideas for Empowering Students to Look at Things from Different Perspectives

Building a Sense of Community Creativity always risks failure. That's why trust is so important to creative people. In the creative process, trust comes from people working together to build a sense of oneness, a community of sorts (Maxwell 2009, 33). Trust and caring don't just happen; they must be intentionally developed.

Jeanne Gibbs in her book *Reaching All by Creating Tribes Learning Communities* emphasizes that community is the esprit that happens when many minds and hearts come together to work toward a common good. Community happens through inclusion and the appreciation of individual differences (Gibbs 2006, 76).

Creating community requires

- Dedication to resolving rather than avoiding uncomfortable problems and conflicts that begins to separate members.
- Learning and practicing the skills that enable collaboration
- Agreements about how to treat each other
- Time to reflect on how well students are doing building community. (Gibbs 2006, 78).

A positive classroom climate evolves out of

- An atmosphere of trust
- A sense of belonging and community
- Involvement in decision making
- Kindness and encouragement from peers
- The teacher's energy and morale
- The teacher's authenticity and nonjudgmental attitude
- Clear expectations, goals, learning outcomes
- Fairness and equity in participation. (Gibbs 2006, 44)

It is important to choose community building activities geared to the interests, age level, and background of your particular group. Taking time out to build trust and community is not to be limited to the beginning of the year and fillers. They are meaningful and purposeful strategies for creating a sense of unity and need to be continued throughout the year.

Achieving Consensus Everyone can benefit from acknowledging that there are as many ways of seeing the world as there are individuals (Erwin 2010, 100). Consequently, learning how to come to a consensus is vital to becoming a responsible citizen living in a democracy. It's part of everyday life.

Achieving consensus is a process that begins with multiple points of view and ends with mutual agreement. Consensus aligns the power of the group to get things done. A consensus is reached when at least one of the following is achieved:

- The agreement (or decision, solution, or plan) meets or exceeds your needs as well as the needs of each of the other group members.
- The agreement addresses the objective of the discussion.
- Everyone in the group will work to support the agreement. (Scott and Flanigan 1996, 3)

We have included a favorite way to practice the process of coming to a consensus. It is a team-building activity called Alien Task Force. We like it so much we included the entire lesson plan for you to try. (See appendix C for Alien Task Force lesson plan.)

HOW CAN I BECOME A TEACHER WHO USES DIVERGENT THINKING IN MY PRACTICE?

See Divergent Thinking as a Strength

Many students believe that if they are not naturally divergent thinkers, they can never become one. But divergent thinking can be cultivated in the right supportive environment. Students will experiment more in divergent thinking when we, as teachers, promote it. In fact, the biggest stumbling block to divergent thinking is the belief that it may be frowned upon in school or perhaps not permitted at all. When innovation and deep thinking are openly encouraged, students realize they have the go-ahead to think divergently and will do it.

Students need help in learning how to tap their reservoir of originality and liberate their creative potential (Costa & Kallick 2009, 58). For teachers, that means trying new things in new ways. It is being willing to test the pedagogical waters for ideas that are innovative and on the cutting edge of best practice.

Seeing divergent thinking as a strength may be harder for some than for others. It is not the level of difficulty or sense of ease that counts. It is our willingness to offer instruction that promotes divergent thinking, no matter who we are and what we are most familiar with doing.

Teachers who advance divergent thinking value diverse thinking strategies, make time for it, defend it, and assess student growth in it. We help maintain children's motivation and passion for in-depth learning when we promote divergent thinking.

Offer Layered Instruction

Teaching for divergent thinking simply means that teachers strive to develop classroom conditions conducive to it. We must be careful to establish an environment of deep thinking and growth.

We need to peel back the layers of thinking for students to discover their ability to reason divergently. A layered instruction empowers students to dig deep, recognize their capabilities, and practice divergent thinking on a consistent basis. Layered instruction

- Demands that students build their understanding through systematic inquiry (Jackson 2011b, 44).
- Presents ideas that conflict with students' present beliefs and prompts students to seek information that will resolve the conflict (Jackson 2011b, 44).
- Expects students to use evidence to defend opinions and extend meaning.
- Insists on distinguishing important information from supporting and/or interesting details.
- Examines the perspectives of others.
- Provides multiple pathways that lead to understanding.
- Raises questions.
- Helps students make meaning for themselves by manipulating, reorganizing, and adapting what students are learning to novel contexts (Jackson 2011b, 59).
- Withholds information and compels students to fill in the gaps.
- Confronts students to impose order on seeming disorder (Jackson 2011b, 43).
- Generates alternative strategies for solving problems.
- Exposes students to multiple possibilities for problem solving.

- Helps students systematize new learning for future use (Jackson 2011b, 59).

Put Students in Critical, Divergent Thinking Situations

Curiosity, creativity, and divergent thinking processes are stimulated by learning tasks of optimal difficulty, relevancy, authenticity, challenge, and novelty for each student (Gibbs 2006, 62). We have included some available resources to assist you in creating critical, divergent thinking situations.

Problem-based learning resources:

- http://www.udel.edu/inst/
- http://www.lessonplanet.com
- http://www.ncsu.edu/pbl/
- http://iae-pedia.org/Good_PBL_Lesson_Plans
- http://www.indiana.edu/~oso/inq.htm

Project based instruction resources that provide students with the intrinsic rewards of natural curiosity and a search for meaning (Ronis 2006):

- http://www.learningreviews.com/Project-Based-Learning.html
- http://www.coloradoadulted.org/SS%20Lessons%20for%20Adult%20Learners/Curriculum%20Topics/lessontemplate.pdf
- http://pbl-online.org/
- http://kidseducationalwebsites.blogspot.com/2011/01/project-based-learning-lesson-plans.html

Experiential learning resources:

- http://wilderdom.com/experiential/
- http://njaes.rutgers.edu/learnbydoing/weblinks.html
- http://www.aee.org/

Cross-curricular and cross disciplinary studies (one of the most exciting benefits is that the integration of disciplines into themes enhances the pattern-seeking operation of the brain, which in turn increases intelligence [Gibbs 2006, 55]):

- http://www.eduplace.com/rdg/res/vogt.html
- http://www.netc.org/focus/strategies/them.php
- http://www.pdesas.org/

LIFELONG LEARNERS ARE DIVERGENT THINKERS

If a man does not keep pace with his companions, perhaps it is because he hears a different drummer. Let him step to the music he hears, however measured or far away.

—Henry David Thoreau, *Walden* (1854)

"Walking to the beat of a different drummer." We have all used this phrase to describe a certain student. We admit, however, that using this statement to describe a student wasn't always meant as a compliment, but more of a complaint.

Neuroscience studies tell us that the chemistry and cognitive brain structures of today's children have evolved, enabling them to learn in very different ways (National Institute of Mental Health 2011). For our students to succeed in the twenty-first century, we must provide an environment that is conducive to not only walking to a different beat but also to creating new beats for others to follow. Who else but our students will possess the inventiveness necessary to produce a low-cost, but environmentally safe alternative fuel source; generate ideas to stop hunger; fashion new technology in an ever-changing world; discover a cure for cancer; or offer a means to achieve peace? We need visionaries to become our future leaders. For that to happen, we call for divergent thinkers.

5

Lifelong Learners Are Self-Efficacious

The outer conditions of a person's life will always be found to reflect their inner beliefs.

—James Lane Allen

WHAT IS SELF-EFFICACY?

Psychologist Albert Bandura has defined self-efficacy as the "belief in one's capabilities to organize and execute the course of action required to manage prospective situations" (Bandura 1995, 2). Being self-efficacious refers to the confidence one has in one's ability to positively affect conditions in life in order to bring about a positive result.

Self-efficacy is an optimistic evaluation of one's capacity to cope with a given situation. It is a sense of personal power. People with high self-efficacy believe they have control of their own lives—that their own actions and decisions have an effect on what they do and who they become. They are more willing to participate in life's experiences because they feel they have some influence on the outcome. On the other hand, people with low self-efficacy see their lives as out of their hands. They avoid challenging tasks altogether for fear of failure.

Efficacious people are open to trying new experiences because they have faith in being able to contribute something to them. If the experience doesn't work out as planned, they use it as a learning experience and move on. Efficacious people find a bright side.

Self-efficacious people:

- Welcome challenges.
- Develop a deeper interest in activities.
- Believe they have the resources necessary to be successful.
- Think their contributions make a difference.
- Expect things to work out for the best.
- Are self-motivated.
- Surround themselves with positive people.
- Choose to think good thoughts.
- Are willing to learn something new.
- Form a strong sense of commitment to their interests and activities.
- Recover quickly from setbacks and disappointments.
- Remain hopeful.

People with a low sense of self-efficacy:

- Do not believe they have control over outcomes, whether societal or personal.
- Believe that difficult tasks and situations are beyond their capabilities.
- Dwell on personal failings and negative outcomes.
- Quickly lose confidence in personal abilities.
- Are slow to initiate a task due to fear of failure.
- Think that failure is due to ability rather than effort.

WHY IS SELF-EFFICACY IMPORTANT
TO BECOMING A LIFELONG LEARNER?

The future belongs to those who believe in their dreams.

—Eleanor Roosevelt

Yes, these words are inspirational. But when we consider the times in which they were spoken (the Depression, World War II, Hitler's rule), we can truly appreciate the positive impact that someone with a high sense of self-efficacy can make.

We choose our thoughts and actions, even in the face of the strongest hardship. We can allow obstacles to shape us, believing we have no control over the outcome, or we can do whatever is within our power to rise above them. Eleanor Roosevelt understood the power of self-efficacy.

Research shows that self-efficacy influences motivation, learning, and achievement in relationships, academics, and the workplace. Maciejewski, Prigerson, and Mazure found that levels of self-efficacy play a significant role in our interactions well into adulthood. They studied the behaviors of adults in stressful work situations and found that those reporting high amounts of self-efficacy were better able to cope with demanding conditions. Those who reported low levels of self-efficacy found themselves highly stressed and frustrated, which led to decreased productivity and increased signs of depression and instability (Maciejewski, Prigerson, & Mazure 2000, 373).

Research done by Sharon Andrew and Wilma Vialle also shows the connection between self-efficacy and productivity. They found that students with high levels of self-efficacy show an increase in academic performance compared to those who reported low self-efficacy (Andrew & Vialle 1998).

In truth, we are more likely to be motivated when we believe we can be successful and will have a positive effect, as opposed to believing that no matter what we do we will not be successful. If we doubt our competency, we lose interest.

A strong sense of self-efficacy provides the inner strength it takes to strive for more, because success is believed to be within reach (Quate & McDermott 2009, 34). It enhances accomplishment and personal well-being in many ways. People with high self-efficacy maintain strong commitment to personal goals and sustain their efforts in the face of failure. They quickly recover a sense of efficacy after setbacks. They attribute failure to insufficient effort or an incomplete skill set, which are both acquirable, and they approach uncertainty with assurance that they can exercise control over it. Such an efficacious outlook generates more personal success, reduces stress, and reduces vulnerability to depression (Bandura 1994, 71).

SELF-EFFICACY FOSTERS LIFELONG LEARNING

Efficacy-Activated Cognitive Processes

Every word, every deed begins as a thought. As a result, whatever happens next is the product of that thought. Those who have a high sense of efficacy imagine themselves as being capable. Those who doubt their efficacy often dwell on the many things that can go wrong and can basically wait for the "other shoe to drop."

It is difficult to fight through self-doubt. It requires a strong sense of efficacy to remain focused and effective in the face of pressures and setbacks. Indeed, when people are faced with the tasks of managing challenging circumstances, those who are weighed down with doubt about their usefulness begin to spiral downward cognitively, lowering their aspirations. What happens next? The quality of their performance deteriorates.

In contrast, those who maintain a resilient sense of efficacy set challenging goals for themselves and believe they possess the skill set to accomplish those goals. In a sense, people with high self-efficacy "spiral upward" in stressful situations because they know they have succeeded through something like it before and can do it again.

It takes an efficacious spirit to set goals and plan courses of action designed to realize success in accomplishing these goals. Without a doubt, inspiration is first cognitively generated. Motivation and self-efficacy are parallel thoughts. People first form beliefs about what they can do and whether it will make a difference. They anticipate likely outcomes of prospective actions.

Two of Our Favorite Ideas for Empowering Students
to "Spiral Upward" Cognitively

Instilling a Growth Mindset   The growth mindset is based on the principle that our basic qualities are things we can cultivate through our efforts. Although people may differ in every which way—in their initial aptitudes, interests, or temperaments—everyone can change and grow through energy, motivation, and hard work (Dweck 2006, 7). Certainly we will have setbacks and disappointments, but just knowing that effort affects ability can empower us toward growth and possibility. Carol Dweck emphasizes that "we do not have to be held captive by a fear of not being great. We simply need to realize that we are working toward better" (Dweck 2006, 8).

Teachers should help students, especially at-risk learners, to link successes to their effort and hard work. When teachers do this, the students develop self-efficacy and the confidence that they have the power within themselves to be successful (Tileston 2010a, 37). If students think that successes are due to effort and if they see themselves as hard working, they will persist longer.

Modeling for students the importance of preparation and effort helps develop a growth mindset. Through it, students learn they can grow smarter with the right kind of preparation and commitment.

Isn't it ironic that students usually limit the importance of exercise and hard work to success in sports? They believe achievement in school can only come from innate ability. "He's just smart" or "I'm not good at math." We need to change that mindset and bring the playing field mentality of "No pain, no gain" into academics. There is great power, lifelong effects, in knowing that hard work pays off. Let students in on this. Having a growth mindset provides us with the hope we need to persevere in all of life's situations. Thankfully, we are not finished products. We can become smarter, better human beings with effort and dedication.

Carol Dweck, in her book *Mindset: The New Psychology of Success*, recommends the following ideas for teachers to instill a growth mindset in their students:

- Praise students for the work and effort they put into something. Pay attention to the messages you give about success. Instead of the "You're so smart and you're a natural" messages, try saying "You really studied for that test and it paid off. Congrats!" or "I really admire how you stuck with your project even when it got difficult. You should be very proud of your efforts." This affords the growth mindset message that everyone can improve with hard work.
- Reassure students that they have control over their performance on a test. That control comes through effort and hard work. Model how to study, take notes, and prepare for a big test. Then let students relax, knowing they've done everything in their control to do well.

- Provide messages that treat failure as a learning lesson. Everyone will fail at some point. That is not important. What is important is how they react to that failure. Protecting them from failure is not helping them grow as individuals. Let them feel it, then facilitate a concrete plan with them to use the failure as a learning opportunity for growth. Failing at something is not the end of the world, and it certainly does not mean we are failures. (Dweck 2006, 173–74)

Promoting "Possibility Thinking" Possibility thinking means seeing the potential for growth in every situation—it's looking for positive possibilities despite the circumstances. When we act on good thoughts, we recognize the promise in them enough to move forward. John Maxwell, in *How Successful People Think*, establishes that to be successful, we must learn to recognize the possibilities in life. Possibility thinkers not only appreciate all that life offers, but they also see their own contributions to life as valuable.

Maxwell emphasizes that "It doesn't take a genius IQ or twenty years of experience to find the possibility in every situation. All it takes is the right attitude, and anybody can cultivate that" (Maxwell 2009, 68). To boot, possibility thinking is contagious. We can't help but become more confident and think bigger when we're around possibility thinkers.

John Maxwell lists the following benefits of possibility thinking:

- Possibility thinking draws opportunities and people to you.
- Possibility thinking gives you energy.
- Possibility thinking keeps you from giving up.
- Possibility thinking brings about success. (Maxwell 2009, 61)

Carol Dweck agrees that possibility thinking transforms potential: "For twenty years my research has shown that the view you adopt for yourself profoundly affects the way you lead your life" (Dweck 2006, 6).

As teachers, we can foster possibility thinking by utilizing any of the following ideas:

- *"Really, what's the worst that could happen?"* This one question challenges students to realize the potential in taking positive risks.

For example, a teenager wants to run for student council but is very apprehensive. Truthfully, what's the worst that could happen? He or she loses the election? That's doable. What is gained from the experience far outweighs that loss. When students ask, "Really, what's the worst that could happen?" it provides the venue for seeing the positives that can come out of taking a risk. Teachers should use this question as part of their teaching dialogue. Share times in your life when you may have used it to propel you past fear to new heights.

- *"I can't means I won't."* Post it, refer to it, and challenge students to live by it. No excuses. Students are more inclined to take a risk if they believe they can succeed and generally avoid tasks where their self-efficacy is low. It is a fact that some things take more effort than others, but we still can give it a go. And teachers are not exempt. The more we share our possibility thinking with students, they more they'll follow suit.

- *Transformative thinking.* Students need to know from day one that what matters most is that they give their strongest effort consistently. The ball is in their court. The road to success begins with a personal decision to invest. There are no shortcuts. We cannot pretend we don't know that people without diplomas end up in low-paying jobs. We all must gain the skills of engaging in self-directed learning if we want to succeed in life. We are playing for keeps—taking school seriously from day one opens doors. The ramifications of ignorance pertain to everyone. Let students in on this. Be transparent about the connection between valuing education and effort, and the payoff from it.

- *Find inspiration in other "possibility thinkers."* Study the lives of great achievers you admire. You will discover they were possibility thinkers. How about Robert F. Kennedy, for example? He gave a passionate testimonial in seeing life's possibilities when he shared, "Some men see things as they are and ask, why? I dream of things that never were and ask, why not?"

WHAT DOES IT TAKE TO BECOME SELF-EFFICACIOUS?

The extent to which individuals believe they have the resources, ability, or power to change a situation is critical to their future success (Tileston

2010a, 21). Our perception of ourselves in relation to the world around us is shaped by whether or not we believe we have some control over our circumstances, whether we believe that we can influence positive change—our sense of self-efficacy. A self-efficacious person understands that effort and hard work stimulate motivation and accomplishment.

How can we cultivate self-efficacy? For that answer we go to the father of the self-efficacy movement, Albert Bandura. He attests that one's sense of self-efficacy begins to form in early childhood as one deals with varied backgrounds, understandings, and situations. However, the growth of self-efficacy does not end during youth but continues to evolve, as a person acquires new skills, experiences, and insights (Bandura 1992).

According to Bandura, there are four major sources of self-efficacy.

1. Providing Mastery Experiences

We must first believe we possess the resources, ability, and power to be successful if we are going to thrive in this world, and one of the biggest influences on self-efficacy is feeling success. Simply put, success raises self-efficacy, and failure lowers it.

Even young children need to experience success in order to maintain it. Experiencing some success provides the inner emotional strength to strive for more, because it is within reach. Driven forward by that optimism, self-efficacious children keep on trying hard, and that effort gives way to more mastery experiences. This "win–continue to win cycle" empowers children to grow to be highly effective and productive in school.

All students need to see themselves as capable learners. Consequently, as their teachers, we need to provide ample time when all students see themselves as scholars (Keene 2008, 55). The old adage "Success breeds success" is absolutely true. Providing opportunities for students to experience success in incremental steps increases their self-efficacy. Recognizing incremental steps toward success is the best way to nurture it. Once a student takes the first step toward investing, the steps that follow are much easier (Tileston 2010a, 21). Continued achievement is more attainable when students' first efforts in working toward their goals are met with success. Robyn Jackson stresses that "If we want students to take more than one step toward success, we have to acknowledge that first step" (Jackson 2011b, 100).

Two of Our Favorite Ideas for Empowering Students
to Increase Self-Efficacy through Experienced Success

Nothing Succeeds like Success: Strengthening Your Students'
Strengths Three-time teacher of the year Alan Sitomer says, "Body-builders don't acquire new biceps; they vigorously exercise the ones they already have until each muscle ripples." The same philosophy applies to learning (Sitomer 2008, 90). Students need to be trained in how to strengthen their strengths. For this to transpire, we have to tap into our students' talents and strengths that already exist. That means taking the time to identify and understand what students bring to the table and letting them in on it. By naming what students do well, teachers validate that they are capable of success, providing an "If I can do it here, I can do it there" mindset that is essential for continued success. That alone will carry your students well beyond the classroom.

When we operate from the platform of looking at strengths first, we are literally changing the learning state of a classroom. We should focus on what students *can* do, instead of just identifying what they *can't* do (Tileston 2010b, 80).

What's our advice here? Draw upon and highlight the contributions that each student brings to the learning. Look for what students do well, especially for struggling students. When students feel capable, they believe in themselves and in turn become even more capable. Here you will find several simple, but very effective ways to strengthen your students' strengths:

- *"Expert at . . ."* At the beginning of each year, survey your students (or a parent for little ones). Find out what their interests are, what they're good at, and what they would like to learn. Save these and use them at opportune times in the learning. Award each student the title "Expert at . . ." Other students can utilize the experts as resources. Some teachers create a class book of "Yellow Pages" so students know who the experts are for certain topics and talents.
- *"My Learning Timeline" or autobiography.* Challenge students to create a timeline or autobiography of their life as a student. Ask them to include the high points and their struggles. Discover what they attribute to the times when they were most successful. Draw upon this information when creating lessons.

- *Get to know your students.* Take the time to listen to what your students enjoy, how they spend their spare time, what they feel they are best at. Bring this up in a positive way in the learning.
- *Provide choice.* Students will be more able to show their strengths when you provide options for them. (More about the power of choice later.)
- *Notice their efforts.* When you take the time to notice a student's hard work, that effort will more than likely be repeated. Everyone feels good about being recognized for a job well done.

Shrinking the Change   In their book *Switch: How to Change Things When Change Is Hard*, Mike and Dan Heath propose that one way to motivate action is to make people feel closer to the finish line than they might have thought. According to research, people find it more motivating to be partly finished with a longer journey than to be at the starting gate of a shorter one (Heath & Heath 2010, 127).

If students are facing a daunting task and their instinct is to avoid it, you've got to break down the task and shrink the change. Make the change small enough that they can't help but score a victory (Heath & Heath 2010, 134). Shrinking the change is a significant approach to help students make an initial commitment.

The ideas to shrink the change in your classroom are endless. Here are just a few ideas that work very well:

- Preteach a challenging lesson with a study group (either voluntary attendance or special invitation as a needs-based group). Then when you introduce the lesson with the whole class, the study group is already familiar with the work. What a great way to build and activate background knowledge.
- Offer study sessions before or after school and give an extra credit point for attending.
- Frontload by engaging students in the upcoming learning. Supply definitions for difficult vocabulary they will need to understand the lesson, or engage them emotionally to pique their interest around an upcoming theme or study.

- Hold an impromptu study session during class time immediately before a test. Include two of the actual problems from the test without the students knowing. Share strategies and the thinking behind each. When you hand out the test, show the student the two problems they've already done and let everyone know they've all gotten full credit for those problems. This is classic shrinking the change, and it works wonders to increase students' self-efficacy.
- Cut your assessments into doable parts. Give students the first three questions of a test. When those questions are completed correctly, hand out either the remainder of the test or another chunk to be completed.
- Chunk your projects into manageable parts and have frequent check-in opportunities.
- Give students the opportunity to chunk their own projects in a way that works for them.
- Have students write questions they still have about the learning. Afford "study buddy" time the day before a test during the last ten minutes of class. Circulate around the room and provide necessary feedback.
- Make a section of your tests take-home or "solve with a partner."
- Offer several questions to choose from on tests and/or assignments.
- Provide study guides and count them toward the test grade.
- Include one or two of the exact questions on a study guide that will be on the test.
- Give one or two of the most difficult questions on a test ahead of time. Let students solve them either at home or with a partner. Then attach the completed work to the test.
- Allow your students to represent the learning using their strengths.

Don't get us wrong: we support raising the bar. But every now and then, we have to know when to lower it for a moment. The power comes when students aren't even aware you helped them out. They feel better about themselves as learners. We used to think of it as "going one step backward to get two steps ahead." But to tell you the truth, shrinking the change is not going backwards at all. It's providing the wings necessary for students to soar ahead on their own.

2. Social Modeling

In all stages of human development, behavior is learned through observation. A behavior is performed by one person and observed by another. The observer then chooses to dispose of the information or code it for future use.

Teachers can take advantage of the influence behind social modeling by building it into daily instruction. Students need to see how you and other perhaps more successful students behave in stressful situations, problem solve, manage their time, or complete a task. Struggling students benefit from hearing and seeing how a more successful student works, especially when the learning gets challenging. Albert Bandura indicates that seeing people similar to oneself succeed by sustained effort raises observers' beliefs that they too possess the capabilities to master comparable activities to succeed (Bandura 1994).

Two of Our Favorite Ideas for Empowering Students
to Increase Self-Efficacy through Social Modeling

Mixed-Ability Problem-Solving/Planning Partner Sessions When you have a clear picture of the abilities of your students (through observing, test scores, problem-solving capabilities, personal strengths, etc.), create mixed-ability partners. These groups should remain intact for at least six weeks.

Several times during the week, provide occasions for partners to meet. They can solve a problem together, with each student thinking aloud the processes and procedures for solving the problem. Make sure these moments are nonthreatening and noncompetitive, or you may have the stronger student just do all the work, which defeats the goal of social modeling.

Assign one partner to take the lead on the problem, sharing his or her thoughts in planning. Include an advance organizer for the other student to track the thinking he or she hears during the think aloud. Provide an "echo problem-solving" opportunity for the observing student to retrace the thinking behind the modeling student's problem-solving strategies. Then they can switch roles. This is a great way for students to record and try what it takes to apply good critical thinking skills. One may take the lead and the other may listen, but they both learn.

Another idea is to provide partner planning sessions. In these moments, partners share their goals for accomplishing a task, communicate ideas on managing their time successfully through a project, brainstorm ideas on a writing piece or a research paper, study for an upcoming test, or plan a workable schedule for succeeding through a long-term assignment. It is critical to clarify how these sessions benefited each student and what they accomplished through working together.

Mixed-ability partnerships reinforce the language and behavior necessary for critical thinking to occur, allowing for an entryway into deeper understanding for all students.

Response Cards   Response cards are a great way to increase participation and promote social modeling. According to David W. Munroe and Jennifer Stevenson in the *Journal of Applied Behavioral Analysis*, "Response cards increase the frequency and accuracy of student responding during whole-class instruction" (Munroe & Stevenson 2009, 795).

Response cards can be used in various ways:

- The teacher asks a question, and the students simultaneously respond by writing the correct answer on a dry erase board or mini chalkboard and holding it up. Students turn and talk with a partner and share the thinking behind their answer.
- The teacher utilizes electronic response cards with the help of an electronic white board.
- The teacher prepares index cards with two possible answers, one answer on each side. Each student receives one card. When the teacher asks a question, the students simultaneously hold up the answer and share with a partner the thinking behind their answer.
  - Example: Preprint responses "potential energy" and "kinetic energy." Give one card to each student. Display images and have students identify the energy displayed by holding up the appropriate answer. Have students share the reasoning behind their choice with a partner.

Response cards are also an excellent formative assessment. You can easily see who has mastered the learning and who needs a little help. If there seems to be a lot of hesitation when answering, it is a good indication that you may want to step back and revisit the concept.

3. Social Persuasion

Bandura also avowed that people could be persuaded to believe they have the skills and capabilities to succeed (Bandura 1995). Getting verbal encouragement from others helps people overcome self-doubt and propels them forward. Think about a time when someone encouraged you or acknowledged a job well done. Sometimes that is all we need to push on and succeed.

Social persuasions relate to encouragements or discouragements we receive from another person. They have a very strong influence on us. Isn't it true that most people remember times when something was said that significantly altered their confidence?

While positive persuasions increase self-efficacy, negative persuasions decrease it. Anyone working with children understands this. Good social modeling needs a little push at times. As teachers, we ought to notice star potential in every student, some way, somehow. All students love their moment in the spotlight. If truth be told, who doesn't?

Two of Our Favorite Ideas for Empowering Students
to Increase Self-Efficacy through Social Persuasion

Celebrations

Celebrate what you want to see more of.

—Thomas J. Peters

Taking the time to appreciate critical thinking, good planning, a kindness shared, or effective use of the qualities of a lifelong learner will result in more critical thinking, good planning, kindness, and effective use of the qualities of a lifelong learner. It's that simple.

Celebrations, when they become part of the regular classroom rituals, enhance a caring environment. They model a positive attitude toward learning by focusing on the strengths of the groups and individual students and bring ability to the forefront rather than deficiency (Quate & McDermott 2009, 111).

Csikszentmihalyi confirms that when there is a reason to think that we are appreciated, satisfaction is usually high (Csikszentmihalyi 1990, 113). Recognizing, appreciating, and honoring students for their accomplishments, especially their hard work, will motivate them to exert more than enough energy to continue that success.

We can't always expect students to notice the good things that are happening in the classroom, let alone imitate them. We need to be explicit about what we are celebrating, why it is noteworthy, and how others can use it to benefit themselves.

Celebrations need to be well earned and authentic. They need to be grounded in hard work that leads to genuine accomplishment. If they are contrived, they are not only meaningless, but they can be seen as insulting (Costa & Kallick 2009, 47).

As teachers, we need to be especially careful not to celebrate mediocrity. Students will discount celebrating something they know is lacking. Doing this will come back and "bite you" every time, even if your intentions are good.

There are so many benefits of celebrating student effort and hard work. Here are just a few:

- Celebrations show students they matter.
- Celebrations are fun.
- Celebrations influence behavior in a positive way.
- Celebrations create a sense of community.
- Celebrations increase a sense of self-efficacy.

We need to celebrate moments of success—academically, socially, and personally—for student groups and individuals. Celebrations come in many forms:

1. Whole class events celebrating the culmination of a unit of study (e.g., a coffeehouse, a poetry slam, parent night, science fair, virtual field trip, etc.).
2. Small group celebrations of a job well done through assemblies, on-the-spot recognition, or praise given during class meetings or whole group reflections.
3. Individual celebrations through calls home, notes written, and public recognition. Jeanne Gibbs recommends having two hats available in the classroom; one labeled "Praiser" and the other labeled "Encourager." Students who wear these hats have the job of circulating

throughout the room, discovering the good things their peers are doing and giving appreciation statements (Gibbs 2006, 167).

One of the Things I Love about You . . .

- This is a great activity to do anytime, especially the day before Valentine's Day. (This day works because the students know and respect each other by this point in the school year, and because everyone deserves a little extra love around this time.)
- Ahead of time, decorate a blank piece of computer paper with the title, "One of the things I love about you . . . " Hand them out and have each student write their first names landscape style, written neatly and big. Don't tell them why.
- As their teacher, take the papers home that night and write one sincere compliment about each person on their paper, graffiti style. Be especially thoughtful because the students will use your compliments as a springboard for their own.
- The next day, on Valentine's Day, have students sit in a circle. Give back the papers with your comments on them. Give students a minute to enjoy your comments.
- Explain that each of us has wonderful and unique qualities about them, and today is time to celebrate "one thing I love about you."
- Here is a very important part: the power of this activity is in the set-up. Ask students to look around and silently think of one positive characteristic that represents each person. Give a few examples. Include the qualities of a lifelong learner in some of your compliments. Share how so and so is very tenacious, dependable, loves learning, and so on. This will provide some helpful hints in case someone gets stuck on what to write.
- Announce that all comments are to be appropriate and thoughtful. Otherwise, it is hurtful and that is inexcusable.
- Now have students pass their papers to the left and add a positive comment about each student. Provide a moment for thoughtful reflection before passing the papers again. Keep passing and reflecting until you receive your own paper back. It is more fun if you direct the passing.

• Give students time to read all the wonderful things about themselves. You will see plenty of smiles. Laminate these papers if you can. They are keepers!

4. Psychological Responses

Our emotions affect our sense of self-efficacy, and conversely, our level of efficacy influences our responses to stress. When we are anxious or worried, we are less likely to feel empowered, confident, and in control. Even so, self-efficacious people interpret stressful situations differently. Those with low self-efficacy may think that the nervous feelings are a sign of inability, while those with high self-efficacy interpret these feelings as to be expected and unrelated to their ability to perform. People with increased self-efficacy view stress as a natural part of life and therefore do not allow emotions to take them down.

People can improve their sense of self-efficacy by learning ways to reduce stress and change their frame of mind when dealing with adverse situations.

*Two of Our Favorite Ideas for Empowering Students
to Increase Self-Efficacy through Psychological Responses*

Put a Fence around It   Worrying and anxiety are rampant for little ones. This strategy allows students to learn to self-regulate and even delay thoughts that may be interfering with their ability to concentrate.

1. Identify the worry and/or distracting thought. Write it down on a little slip of paper or for little ones, draw it.
2. Model how to put a fence around the worry or distracting thought by drawing brackets around it.
3. Place the paper in your pocket and give yourself permission to worry about it later. Get back to work.
4. Think aloud through the process. Show students that most of the time, when you revisit the worry later, it doesn't seem to really be that big of a deal.

5. After practicing the above steps, move your students away from writing to being able to create "mental fences" around distracting thoughts and save them for later.

Model How You Handle Stress   Model explicitly for students what you do to relieve stress. Share a stressful situation you are experiencing. Reveal how it makes you feel and what you do with those feelings so as not to shut down. Bring in other adults who work in very stressful circumstances. Have them share their tricks for staying calm, positive, and teachable through challenges. Your students will appreciate knowing that everyone, even you, experiences doubts and fears. Let them see how to get through stressful situations with dignity and grace and become a stronger person as a result.

Use the list of Top Ten Ways to Reduce Stress for Students that follows. This list is a banner for life. Display it as a poster, make a copy for each student, create bookmarks of it, and model how you use it to self-regulate your stress levels during the everyday stressers of life in the classroom.

Top Ten Ways to Reduce Stress for Students

1. *Talk yourself through it. Everyone experiences stress. You can get through it.* Tell yourself this too shall pass.
2. *Silence the negative self-talk.* The second something negative comes in your mind, shut it down. You don't have to listen to ugly talk. Find some positive replacement behavior or mantra to counteract the negativity the moment your brain goes negative. Truth is, most of what we worry about never really happens. Then we used all that energy listening to nonsense, worry, and fear. Imagine all the fun we miss doing that.
3. *Use visual imagery.* Close your eyes and imagine for a minute your favorite place to be. Take a few friends on your virtual trip if you want to. Can you see how much fun you are having and how relaxed you feel? This will help calm you down.
4. *Don't take yourself so seriously.* We make mistakes. We all look the fool at times. Laugh. It's funny. What is happening is not end of the world. In fact, one day you will find it quite hilarious that you took it so seriously. Enjoy your moments—*now.*

5. *Breathe deep.* Close your eyes and take deep, slow breaths. Inhale and visualize exhaling any negativity. Pay attention to your breath for a couple of minutes. Imagine your neurons calming down and your body relaxing because of it. Do this routinely and intentionally.

6. *Exercise.* While in school, you can get the adrenaline going by stretching, standing up, sharpening your pencil, shaking your arms, or taking a quick bathroom break. At home, try a few relaxation poses whenever you are feeling anxious—the best ones for kids are the child's pose (for getting your body at rest), downward facing dog (for relieving fatigue and worry), and extended leg pose (for calming the mind).

7. *Use past practice.* Hey, bet you survived something similar to what you're feeling right now. In fact, it was probably worse, and you got through it. If you did it there, you can do it anywhere. Remember your past successes.

8. *Forgive yourself.* Everyone blows it sometimes. Move on. Get over it. Forgive yourself and others. Life is way sweeter that way.

9. *Call in a friend.* Sharing helps reduce stress. If you're at school, find a good time and talk to a trusted friend.

10. *Eat right.* Healthy foods make us feel better, physically and emotionally. There is great truth in the old adage, "You are what you eat."

HOW CAN I BECOME A TEACHER WHO PROMOTES SELF-EFFICACY IN MY PRACTICE?

Remain Self-Efficacious in Your Ability to Reach All Students

Teachers with a strong sense of self-efficacy believe they can create a vision for all students. Difficult students do not intimidate them because they are confident in their own abilities.

Self-efficacious teachers believe in the power of their own capacity to get through to all types of students. Robyn Jackson confirms that "master teaching means understanding that expectations say more about your own sense of self-efficacy than they do about your students' abilities" (Jackson 2009, 85).

Jackson challenges us to adopt an unwavering faith in ourselves and the importance of our work. If we believe that what we are doing is possible, then we are more likely to be confident in finding a way to prevail in all situations (Jackson 2009, 91).

Differentiate Instruction So That All Students Can Access the Curriculum and Find an Entry Point to the Learning

Differentiating the instruction can build a context that encourages a sense of competence, increasing student self-efficacy. Differentiating the instruction is a method of teaching that advocates active planning for and attention to student diversity. It is presenting a lesson using different modalities so that every student has an opportunity to be successful. When we provide many pathways to the learning for all students to access it, we are promoting a sense of self-efficacy in our students. Students are given several occasions to succeed. And success breeds success.

Carol Ann Tomlinson describes that on some level, differentiation is just a teacher accepting that students learn in different ways, and responding by doing something about that through delivery of instruction. Tomlinson adds that a more dictionary-like definition is "adapting content, process, and product in response to student readiness, interest, and/or learning profile" (Tomlinson 1999).

Three Ways to Differentiate the Instruction and How That Can Look in Your Classroom

Differentiating Instruction according to Interest
- Offering choice in reading
- Offering choice in project ideas
- Allowing students to choose a working partner (once in a while)
- Creating similar interest groups
- Making learning meaningful by tapping into student interest
- Use I—Searches: allowing students to choose their own research topics
- Using dialogue journals between teacher and student or between peers

- Offering shared-interest reading
- Providing "question" or "idea boxes" for suggestions (teachers can draw from these to develop classroom project ideas or tasks)
- Holding class meetings that include share interests, goals, and plans
- Completing personal profiles (students complete surveys in the beginning of the year—gather information on what the students like, are involved in, and enjoy doing)
- Building shared experiences (they are often the thread that links the students together)
- Keeping tabs on what students are doing outside of class (e.g., asking how the game, concert, etc., went)
- Taking time to expand student interests
- Including what the students care about in the lesson
- Celebrating success (create a bulletin board recognizing student achievement—not just academic, but community service, kindness, sports, band, etc.)

Differentiating Instruction according to Learning Profile
- Using learning style inventories (survey students on learning styles and use that data when planning lessons)
- Being aware of your own learning style and pushing your instruction beyond that comfort zone
- Offering choice according to students' learning profile (e.g., tic-tac-toe model, contracts, menus, etc.)
- Including different modalities of instruction—hit the objective as many different ways as possible. This provides many pathways to the learning
- Considering learning profiles when creating tests. Will some students do better on an alternate assessment?
- Having students create options for authentic assessments (e.g., projects)

Differentiating Instruction according to Readiness
- Using data to impact instruction
- Incorporating small group instruction
- Using both homogeneous and heterogeneous grouping
- Employing flexible grouping

- Including Think-Pair-Share and Turn & Talk as part of daily instruction. This provides support for those who may need a little more processing time. Bouncing ideas back and forth provides deeper conversations into the learning.
- Crafting a cohesive lesson from beginning to end so that every student can be brought to the learning
- Using data to form similar ability groups and mixed-ability groups
- Utilizing data to create differentiated learning centers and work stations
- Having students self-assess their understanding throughout the lesson
- Including some type of formative assessment every fifteen minutes or so, especially during the gradual release of responsibility component of your instruction
- Incorporating tiered assignments
- Using exit tickets to assess and use this to shape instruction

Teach Students How to Take Responsibility for Their Attitude.

Alan Sitomer considers that "hardworking teens with smiles in their hearts will inevitably surpass the achievements of gifted kids with chips on their shoulders most of the time" (Sitomer 2008, 57). We also believe there is a direct correlation between a student's attitude and his or her success academically. We'll go one step further and say that attitude is a strong indication of how a student envisions himself or herself and will be a powerful variable determining his or her future in and out of school.

Isn't it alarming that students often believe their attitude is something beyond their control? We need to teach our students that only they can change their outlook, and changing it starts with knowing it's possible.

We can no longer assume students have learned how to create a positive attitude for themselves. Whenever possible, we need to let students in on the fact that they control their attitude and have the power within themselves to create their outlook to work for them and not against them. Allow students the opportunity to check their attitude and gain the freedom to change it when necessary. Model how keeping a positive attitude through the doldrums takes effort and is difficult even for you, but show them it is well worth the investment.

A good attitude can make all the difference, and your students need to understand they have the power within themselves to create the attitude they need to grow as lifelong learners. Sitomer agrees: "It is amazing how many times an attitude shift is the exact remedy students need in order to solve the most vexing issue in their life" (Sitomer 2008, 59).

LIFELONG LEARNERS ARE SELF-EFFICACIOUS

Believing the dots will connect down the road will give you the confidence you need to succeed.

—Steve Jobs 2011

Steve Jobs was certainly one of the more extraordinary contributors to our global society. While he reflected the essence of self-efficacy, we encounter future innovators each day in our classrooms across communities. Knowing that "success breeds success" empowers us to nurture and guide these apprentices with the tools they need to believe that connecting the dots is possible.

Lifelong Learners See Learning As Valuable

Some see more in a walk around the block than others see in a trip around the world.

—Anonymous

WHAT DOES IT MEAN TO SEE LEARNING AS VALUABLE?

The greatest reward for education is the opportunity to learn. It is learning for the sheer joy of it.

Lifelong learners have an unquenchable thirst for learning. They are fascinated with discovering something new; they are ever curious, excited by the prospects of knowing.

People who value learning see school in a different light. They *pursue* learning, approaching education with intent and passion. Lifelong learners see the potential for growth in every situation and have a greater appreciation for improvement, never passing up a chance to learn more. Learning opportunities are everywhere for the lifelong learner. As a matter of fact, lifelong learners often see value in confusion and want to wrestle through something that is difficult just because they understand the potential for self-growth.

Lifelong learners are not interested in shortcuts. They love learning, think for themselves, and work hard for the sheer joy that comes from the experience. They see mistakes as occasions for learning and actually seek out those teachable moments.

People who see learning as valuable understand they are not learning just information, but also higher-order thinking and social and personal skills—competencies critical to their futures (Gibbs 2006, 151). They think in terms of learning and take ownership for their potential, taking pride in their efforts, regardless of the outcome.

WHY IS SEEING LEARNING AS VALUABLE IMPORTANT TO BECOMING A LIFELONG LEARNER?

Everyone is born with an internal drive to learn. Infants and toddlers are innately motivated to explore and grow as learners. They feel a great sense of accomplishment at every triumph. They are determined to continue learning, pushing themselves beyond the known to unchartered territory once again.

Lifelong learners continue this enthusiasm. They perceive life as a series of lessons to be learned. They use these lessons to impact their own lives and the lives of others. Nelson Mandela, one of the greatest examples of someone who understands the impact that knowledge has on life, relates the significance of learning: "Education is the most powerful weapon which you can use to change the world."

Scientists have discovered that intelligence is not fixed. In reality, most of what we were taught about IQ just isn't true. We can become smarter with effort. Lifelong learners realize this and are driven to stay in the game in order to reap the benefits that self-directed learning provides.

Carol Dweck, author of *Mindset*, emphasizes that "education pays and success in learning is 99% hard work" (Dweck 2006, 80). She confirms that even though we start off with a certain temperament and aptitude toward learning, it is clear that experience, training, desire, and effort can have a positive effect on who we become and where we end up in our career choices (Dweck 2006, 5). We have the capacity to expand our minds, so as to expand our horizons. Students who see school as a place to learn something new and take advantage of the opportunities given to them will grow as lifelong learners and will gain the experience they need to thrive far beyond what they might have accomplished without striving to learn.

Success depends on sound, strong habits, and anyone of any ability can develop them. Every activity in school may not have a great impact in life, but the habits students use to approach these tasks will. When students see learning as valuable, it makes all the difference. The real message is that students are not in school for their parents or teachers, or for anyone else for that matter. They are there to reach their own full potential. Lifelong learners make that happen.

WHAT COGNITIVE PROCESSES FOSTER SEEING LEARNING AS VALUABLE?

1. Making Connections

Eric Jensen, in his book *Introduction to Brain-Compatible Learning*, maintains that in order for learning to be considered significant, it must connect to something the learner already knows. It must activate a learner's existing neural networks. The greater the connections, the more meaningful the learning will be (Jensen 1998, 31). Learning happens when the brain seeks out and catalogues patterns, linking new information to prior knowledge and experiences (Gibbs 2006, 154).

Arthur Hyde agrees when he says that forming the right connections, regardless of the grade level, is crucial to establishing global conceptual development (Hyde 2009, 63). It is magical when a student realizes, "Hey, this is just like. . . ." As teachers, we aspire to make these "lightbulb" moments a habit for students, not just a split second of insight once in a great while.

Three of Our Favorite Ideas for Empowering
Students to Make Connections

Include activities that foster making connections in everyday instructional practices. Three easy, but very worthwhile ideas are provided here.

Concept Circles   Concept circles are circles separated into fourths, with words written in each quarter (Vaca, Vaca & Gove 1987). There are many variations to concept circles. Include words that have a common theme, and ask students to discuss and write about the connections they see among the words. A variation is for student to write the words and challenge other students to find connections. You could also write three words and challenge students to identify the connection, and then add a fourth word that would also fit into the category. Another way is to write three words that belong and one word that doesn't, and challenge students to find the word that doesn't fit in. Make sure students can justify their decisions (Allen 1999). To deepen the critical thinking, have students create their own concept circles, either in pairs or individually. Make sure they justify the reasoning behind their thinking. A younger version of a concept circle is to play "One of these things just doesn't belong here." Allow partners to discuss the connections among the concepts, objects, or pictures. Make sure to promote the language of making neural connections.

Collaborative Annotation   Active participation in the learning needs to be modeled, and students must be given plenty of opportunities to try it on. Collaborative annotation provides practice in comprehension, which very often begins with making connections. Ahead of time, enlarge a one-page article, a page from a textbook, or some interesting piece of text. Make it large enough for students to add reactions and responses to it right on the paper. The purpose is for several children to be able to read and make notes right on the paper. To build a sense of accountability, you can assign each member a color. It would be a good idea to model this first with a read aloud and a think aloud as you respond to the text. Now, pass out either the same article or another one and have the students read and respond silently writing notes. Have students share in their groups, and then do a gallery walk allowing groups to read other collaborative annotations (Daniels & Steineke 2011, 89–93; Beers 2003; Wilhelm 2002).

Using Novelty   Brain research has found that novel input makes the brain allocate nerve cells and stimulate neuronal connections (Jensen 1997). Bringing novelty into your instructional delivery stimulates change in your students' thinking. It forces them to create some sense of order to the unfamiliar, the weird. According to Donna Walker Tileston, teachers need to use novelty to get the brain's attention. The brain likes novelty (Tileston 2010a, 35).

Here are just a few examples of how you can include novelty in your daily practice:

- Role-play something outrageous connected to your curriculum. Get dramatic and don't let the students in on it.
- Create a mystery around your intended purpose.
- Bring in visitors—other faculty or staff, experts in the field, community members who use whatever you are teaching in everyday life.
- Use object lessons.
- Bring in primary sources, artifacts, relics.
- Eat! Food is a great way to form strong connections.
- Dance.
- Sing.
- Perform a reader's, writer's, mathematician's, scientist's, historian's theater.
- Play games—some curriculum based (flashlight tag with vocabulary words on the ceiling) and some just for brain breaks (plunger baseball is a favorite).

2. Understanding

Ellin Keene urges teachers to help students discover the powerful capacity of their own minds, which is, in and of itself, intoxicating (Keene 2008, 104).

Keene affirms that "our goal, as teachers, is to engage children as thinkers from the very earliest stages of their schooling . . . to understand the internal gratification that accompanies in-depth learning about complex issues" (Keene 2008, 80). To accomplish this goal, we must weave into our daily conversations what understanding looks like, feels like, and sounds like.

Grant Wiggins and Jay McTighe offer a definition of what understanding looks like in their "Six Sides of Understanding." When we truly understand, we

1. Can explain
2. Can interpret
3. Can apply
4. Have perspective
5. Can empathize
6. Have self-knowledge (Wiggins & McTighe 2005, 84)

Three of Our Favorite Ideas for
Empowering Students to Reach Understanding

Build formative assessments into your daily instructional practice. Robyn Jackson stresses that checking for understanding throughout the class period gives you an opportunity to see in real time how students are progressing toward mastery and adjust your instruction based on student needs (Jackson 2009, 131).

Bell and Cowie (2000) define formative assessment as a bidirectional process between teacher and student to enhance, recognize, and respond to the learning. Research shows that the effects of formative assessment are one of the most powerful weapons in the teacher's arsenal.

Madeleine Hunters refers to it as "dipsticking," quick tools to frequently monitor students' understanding simultaneously on the same topic during instruction (Jackson 2009, 151). How you check in with students is not what is most important; it is that you are intentionally doing it that matters. We always tell our student teachers that using formative assessment effectively is like cooking a turkey; you must take the temperature of your class about every fifteen to twenty minutes. That temperature will tell you what to do from there.

We have included three of our favorite formative assessment ideas. We have seen both ideas used across grade levels and in all subject areas.

Checking In through Teacher Notebooks   Keep a notebook with a page dedicated to each student. Prepare a clipboard filled with sticky labels and circulate around the room while students work independently, or in centers meeting with students to informally check for understanding, jotting down the day and what you learned from the student. Take each sticker and place in on the appropriate student page in your notebook. Now you have a place to track student growth. Teacher notebooks are also an easy way to keep track that you have checked in with each student (Quate & McDermott 2009, 46).

Choral Response   There are so many ways for you to check for understanding through choral response. You can provide two card options for each student and assess their understanding by asking them to chorally lift up the appropriate card upon questioning. You can give them yes/no cards and do the same. Your students can orally respond together using a thumbs up/thumbs down. They can use electronic clickers or respond chorally using mini-whiteboards. Choral responses are an effective and inviting way to formatively assess the learning, and kids love it!

Constructivism   Constructivism is an approach to learning that engages students in inquiry, discovery, self-directed research, problem-solving, formulation of hypotheses, and evaluation. When learning is active and hands-on, the formation of neural connections is facilitated, and information is much more readily remembered than information learned from an abstract viewpoint in which the teacher is doing the work while the students watch (Gregory & Parry 2006). Janet Allen concludes that when students learn through constructivism, they are much more likely to understand, remember, and apply their learning to other situations (Allen 2000, 123).

Teaching that emphasizes inquiry helps students process and retain information. It leads to self-questioning, deeper thinking, and problem solving. Shelley Harwayne (1992) attests to this when she says, "Students will learn most when the journey is really theirs." Students can only understand what they have themselves constructed. When students are forced to construct their own meaning, the investment is genuine. They strive to understand because they are personally involved in the process.

3. Flow

Mihaly Csikszentmihalyi has spent over thirty years researching the idea of flow. His research looks to those who find pleasure and lasting satisfaction in activities, which he defines as being in a state of flow. According to Czikszentmihalyi, flow occurs most often when you are doing what you really enjoy. It is frequently described as an ecstatic state. As a matter of fact, when flow happens, everything else around seems to fade. People experiencing flow often feel a sense of enlightenment.

In flow, you don't need to go somewhere physically. It is not a place; it is an experience all of us feel at some point when our interest and skills meet the challenges set before us with passion. For some, flow occurs while composing music, or scuba diving, or writing poetry. Flow is an effortless spontaneous feeling we get when we are in our sweet spot. We merge ourselves with what we love. It is a passion.

In education, we can compare flow to true engagement. Ellin Keene describes flow in learning as when "students are not paying attention because you tell them to; they're paying attention because they can't bear to miss something important" (Keene 2008, 206). Carol Dweck emphasizes, "The best gift we can give our students is to teach them to love challenges, be intrigued by mistakes, enjoy effort, and keep on learning" (Dweck 2006, 177).

How does it feel to be in flow?

Czikszentmihalyi presents seven conditions that are present when a person is in flow:

1. Completely involved in what we are doing—focused, concentrated
2. A sense of ecstasy—of being outside everyday reality
3. Great inner clarity—knowing what needs to be done and how well we are doing
4. Knowing that the activity is doable, that our skills are adequate to the task—it is possible but difficult
5. A sense of serenity—no worries about oneself, and a feeling of growing beyond the boundaries of the ego
6. Timelessness—thoroughly focused on the present; hours seem to pass by in minutes
7. Intrinsic motivation—whatever produces flow becomes its own reward (Lillie 2011)

*Two of Our Favorite Ideas for Empowering
Students to Experience Flow*

What's flow got to do with it? We were all created to enjoy life. It is essential to let students in on this. Life is not meant to be humdrum, working forty hours a week in a job we hate. Recognizing when and where we feel flow can be life altering. It is these sweet spots in life that often lead us to our destiny. We believe we are exactly where God wants us to be when we experience a sense of flow. It is where we use our gifts and talents for good and feel great doing it. It is living life to the fullest.

Model for students how and when you realized you were meant to be a teacher. Challenge them to pay attention to when they feel the flow and take notice when you see it happening it in your students.

Where's Your Flow? Show students a short video clip (YouTube or TED Talks—depending on the age of your students) on famous people talking about being in their flow. Challenge students to discover what they think "flow" means from watching the short clip. In small groups, have them generate a definition (even little ones can do this). Then ask them why you might take the time to show this. Let them know that each of us experiences this state of flow—we just need to learn to find out when it's happening. When we are tuned in to when our body experiences flow, we can learn to identify our gifts, and more often our destiny. We really are meant to be happy. Then, bring it up throughout the year so that students can see in themselves when and why they experience a state of flow.

Flow Celebrates Diversity You don't have to be a professional athlete to experience flow. You can be a dentist, social worker, fashion designer, anything. Bring in local professionals who are passionate about their jobs. Let them share the satisfaction they feel from doing the job. Include stories of famous musicians, writers, scientists, and politicians who have influenced the world in some way. They are in their flow zone. There is great freedom in knowing it's okay to follow your heart, especially when your passion seems different than what everyone else wants in life.

WHAT DOES IT TAKE TO SEE LEARNING AS VALUABLE?

"Desire is a source of energy, a passion-generating furnace from which people draw creativity, determination, and oomph" (Sitomer 2008, 134). We concur. Much is accomplished from desire, drive, and determination. To instill that kind of passion for education, one must first establish that learning is personally important.

A lifelong learner is one whose primary goal is to expand his or her knowledge and ways of thinking and investigating the world (Dweck 2006, 187). It takes seeing the qualities of a lifelong learner as a means to a successful future—adopting a teachable spirit, one that is humble enough to admit there is always more to learn. Lifelong learners are action driven. They involve themselves in the learning because that's how they see learning: as *theirs.* They are self-motivated to push past any laziness, fear, or uncertainty in order to grow, both personally and academically.

EXHIBIT THE QUALITIES OF A LIFELONG LEARNER

We asked several people we consider to be highly respected in their careers what it takes to see learning as valuable. They came from very different backgrounds, but they have one thing in common: they continue to learn and grow. We did not mention this book or any of the qualities it takes to be a lifelong learner, and we did not suggest any possible answers. It was amazing—every person mentioned at least one of the qualities in this book as necessary to see learning as valuable. Several mentioned it takes tenacity and dedication. Others included being willing to stop and reflect. Some shared that you have to believe in yourself. Everyone mentioned that you should be a good listener and be willing to work and learn from others. It all makes sense. To see learning as valuable, we need to adopt all the qualities of a lifelong learner.

A TEACHABLE SPIRIT

Benjamin Barber, an eminent sociologist, once said, "I don't divide the world into the weak and the strong, or the successes and the failures. . . . I divide the world into the learners and nonlearners" (Hyatt & Gottlieb 1993, 232).

Being teachable means realizing you don't have all the answers and you can't get all the answers, either. You draw on people, books, and experiences as teachers. You don't always have to be right. In fact, when you are corrected, you don't immediately feel threatened, building a defense. You are teachable and pay attention to the lessons life brings your way. You create opportunities to learn because you value the gift of learning, and you often take the initiative to ask for feedback, using it to improve.

Having a teachable spirit means being open to learning, even when the lessons are hard to accept. Maybe you misjudged, overreacted, or didn't react at all. But you are humble enough to realize that sometimes you are at fault and need to make it right.

Being teachable means seeing life as a set of lessons meant to create a better you, for your own sake and for the sake of others. Stephanie Pace

Marshall (2003) attested to this when she said, "We ourselves have to first become that which we want others to become."

Two of Our Favorite Ideas for Empowering Students to Have a Teachable Spirit

Model a Teachable Spirit Forget about the image of being the "all-knowing teacher." Students see right through that, and it is way too much pressure to uphold. Let your students know you are learning right along with them. Facilitate their learning instead of trying to be the great dispenser of knowledge. It doesn't work. Students will respect you so much more for your transparency and willingness to learn. Modeling a teachable spirit empowers your students to see learning as continuous and worthwhile.

Ask questions when you are confused. Say you don't know, and then model how you search for the answer. Take notice when students are teaching *you* something and thank them for it. Model what it looks like and sounds like to humbly admit when you are wrong. Demonstrate how you search for meaning in these times to better yourself. As Alan Sitomer attests, "It's okay to not know; it's not okay, however, not to search" (Sitomer 2008, 136).

Ask students how you can improve as a teacher and use their advice. Share that you took their advice and improved the next project, assignment, rubric, or assessment to best represent their needs. Your humility during these moments will speak volumes.

You cannot assume all students have good role models at home to show them the benefits of learning. When you take the time to model how to see learning as valuable, you are providing a gift that lasts a lifetime.

Provide Opportunities for Students to Learn from Their Peers Challenge students to pay attention to how they react when you call on another student. Do they listen or simply tune out? Experiment with this; stop at times during a class discussion and prompt students to check their focus and attentiveness whenever their peers answer. Provide an advance organizer encouraging them to paraphrase or summarize the contributions from other students. What important points did they hear? What points do they most agree with? Why? What might they want to add?

Include collaborative teaching techniques that will help students see each other as resources. Simple methods like "think-pair-share" and "turn-and-talk" provide an opportunity for students to practice their thinking out loud. It is beneficial to provide time for students to bounce ideas off each other before holding them accountable for the learning. When students are given time to negotiate meaning, they understand things better.

Active Learner

"Everyone put your thinking caps on." "Be prepared to use your noodle today."

We smile as we write these familiar prompts to learning. As funny as they sound, the message is clear. When we actively pursue learning, we become smarter. According to Carol Dweck, "The brain is more like a muscle—it changes and gets stronger when you use it. And scientists have been able to show just how the brain grows and gets stronger when you learn" (Dweck 2006, 219). Activating your brain begins with actively involving yourself in the learning experience.

When students decide to become active participants in learning, the formation of neural connections is facilitated and information is much more readily remembered than information learned from a passive standpoint, in which the teacher is doing the work while the students watch (Gregory & Parry 2006). Active learners pursue learning. They are drawn to it and realize the ball is in their court when it comes to understanding something.

Our Favorite Idea for Empowering
Students to Become Active Learners

Activate Your Thinking before, during, and after the Learning   We are proponents of having students activate their thinking throughout the learning process. We first learned about before, during, and after (BDA) learning in reading comprehension. We highly recommend using the BDA format in every grade level and every subject. It empowers students to become cognitively involved in the learning from beginning to end.

There are endless resources for implementing BDA learning as part of your instructional practice. Jim Burke's "103 Things to do Before/During/After Reading" is very worthwhile (Burke 1998).

Jeff Zwiers suggests using the following BDA comprehension prompts with students:

BEFORE reading, I . . .
- ✓ Know the purpose of reading
- ✓ Use pre-reading techniques
- ✓ Think about what I already know about this topic
- ✓ Make predictions about what I think the text will tell me

DURING reading, I . . .
- ✓ Stop to visualize, summarize parts, ask questions, and organize thought
- ✓ Reread parts I don't understand
- ✓ Predict and then confirm or change my predictions
- ✓ Figure out unknown words by using the words around them and word parts
- ✓ Organize information with notes or drawings

AFTER reading, I . . .
- ✓ Write a quick summary of the reading in my learning log to remember it
- ✓ Go back and look at the notes I made to organize them
- ✓ Think about how the reading relates to classroom learning and life
- ✓ Reflect on what I read (Zwiers 2004, 185)

In appendix D, there are samples of how the BDA format is used to help students hold their thinking while navigating through informational texts.

Kinesthetic Learning

Multisensory teaching makes sense. Children love to explore. They want to move, get their hands dirty, and discover new things. It's what makes children, children.

Instructional situations that involve the use of movement necessitate more sensory input than do situations requiring only worksheets (Gregory & Parry 2006). Every time we move our bodies, our brains release acetylcholine. This neurotransmitter stimulates the brain and yields new synaptic growth. The neural pathways become stronger (S. Jones 2003).

The brain fuels itself on the oxygen in the blood that is produced by physical activity (Sousa 2006).

Again, the options for getting students up and moving are endless. Students can create songs and perform them, create Double Dutch chants while jumping rope, create body formations in groups, write and perform skits and commercials—all around your learning purpose.

A change in stimuli is crucial, since the amount of time a student can focus is equivalent to the age of the student in minutes (Sylwester 2000). Neurologist and middle school teacher Judy Willis (2009) says that if instruction doesn't change delivery styles every twenty minutes, dopamine levels significantly drop in the brain. The brain needs dopamine to absorb new information.

Two of Our Favorite Ideas for Empowering Students through Kinesthetic Learning

Kagan structures are very successful in using movement within the context of your curriculum. We are including two of our favorite structures that promote kinesthetic learning here. Each structure listed has is tried and true across both grade levels and curriculum. You can find many more ideas at http://www.KaganOnline.com.

Line-Ups   This page has been copied with permission from Kagan Publishing & Professional Publishing, 2009, 1(800)933-2667. http://www.KaganOnline.com.

USE: Classbuilding, Higher-Level Thinking, Mastery, Comparing and Ordering, Sequencing Events in History, Identifying Plot

PURPOSE: All or most students are engaged while reviewing a concept, comparing and ordering, sequencing events in history, identifying plot, or learning more about each other.

DIRECTIONS:

1. Teacher creates cards ahead of time. You can create cards for small groups to line up or enough for the whole class.
2. Teacher announces and distributes the cards.
3. Students line up by positioning themselves according to the directives. Students can also be challenged to come up with an order without the directive.

4. Come to a consensus. Pairs or whole class discuss order and make any necessary corrections.

Mix-N-Match This page has been copied with permission from Kagan Publishing & Professional Publishing, 2009, 1(800)933-2667. http://www.KaganOnline.com.

USE: Classbuilding, Mastery, Vocabulary Development, Increasing Mental Stamina

PURPOSE: All students are engaged while reviewing a concept, promoting vocabulary development, increasing mental stamina, or learning more about each other.

DIRECTIONS:

1. Teacher prepares cards. Every card has another card that matches it in some way (e.g., conversions, definitions, famous person along with their particular achievement in history or science, pictures with a definition, etc.).
2. Distribute cards.
3. Students mix around and trade cards with at least three people.
4. Teacher calls "Freeze."
5. Students find their "Match." After they match-off, have them form a big circle around the outside of your room. You can time this and have each class try to beat their own time, or you can make it a competition among the classes.

Self-Motivated to Learn

Students who see learning as valuable take charge of motivating themselves. They are not content with mere memorization. As Carol Dweck puts it, "They study to learn, not just to ace a test" (Dweck 2006, 61). If they are confused, they use it to motivate themselves through the struggle to find clarity.

Self-motivated students stay engaged and positive. Even when things are boring, those who value learning try to make it more interesting. They understand that being motivated keeps them focused and ready to learn, so they want to stay motivated and do not depend on anyone to do it for them.

Self-motivated students do not believe test scores alone tell them what their potential is, what they are capable of, what their future holds. They will not be pigeonholed by such things. They believe abilities can be cultivated and so they keep trying.

Two of Our Favorite Ideas for Empowering Students to Become More Self-Motivated

Consequence Thinking   Students need to know from day one that what matters most is that *they* give their strongest effort *consistently*. Learning is a choice, and there are consequences for those choices. Quite honestly, the ball is in *their* court.

The road to success begins with a personal decision to invest. There are no shortcuts. We cannot pretend that people without diplomas end up in high-wage jobs. In order to succeed in life, we must learn what it takes to become a self-directed learner. We are playing for keeps—taking school seriously opens doors. The ramifications of ignorance pertain to everyone.

The truth is that education pays. Alan Sitomer agrees. "Let students know that if they don't know how to properly read a set of directives, distinguish the real meaning behind the message in a household mailer, or comprehend and evaluate critical information, they risk the chance of being duped by false advertising, missing out on a fantastic deal that could have saved them a lot of money, or entering into a contractual arrangement in which they agree to things they have no idea they are agreeing to" (Sitomer 2008, 65).

As John Dewey put it, "Education is life, not a preparation for life." Talk directly to your students about the connection between valuing education, effort, and its eventual payoff.

Learning to Care   How do we get students to care about their learning? This is the one question that has plagued teachers for years. Ruth Charney (2002) believes the answer is in teaching children to first care for themselves, their fellow students, and their environment, and then they are more capable of being concerned about academics. Where do we begin? By realizing that in order for students to thrive academically, they first need to feel cared for, accepted, and appreciated as valued members of the classroom community.

Cohen acknowledges that virtually all learning happens within the context of human relationships (Cohen 1999, 17). The time spent on teaching children to care is not wasted time. It builds the foundation necessary for learning to flourish. Rarely can we, as humans, grow in an environment where we don't feel cared for, appreciated, or accepted. The time it takes to model what it looks like and sounds like to care for something or someone is worth it.

Teaching students to care is a worthwhile investment. Students who feel a sense of respect and responsibility tackle their schoolwork with more conviction, whereby both teachers and students experience more success

Paula Denton and Roxann Kriete recommend a slow and deliberate start to the academic curriculum. They assert that beginning the school year with a strong emphasis on teaching and modeling respect and responsibility, as well as creating a sense of community will

1. Build a solid foundation of trust and warmth between the teachers and children and among the children.
2. Give children many opportunities to model, role-play, and practice expected behaviors in order to be successful.
3. Create an environment where it is safe to take risks, make mistakes, and work to fix mistakes.
4. Nurture and extend each child's sense of belonging to a group, of being an important contributor to the group, and of needing the group.
5. Nurture each child's ability to exercise independence and responsibility in work, care for materials and care for others.
6. Excite and motivate children to the potentials of learning in their classroom environment (Denton & Kriete 2000, 4).

HOW CAN I BECOME A TEACHER WHOSE PRACTICE AND PEDAGOGY EXEMPLIFIES SEEING LEARNING AS VALUABLE?

Keeping It Relevant

For twenty-first-century learners, working toward good grades is no longer enough to keep them in the game. Students long for a sense of

purpose. They crave validation. Just look at the popularity of social net-
working sites. As Robyn Jackson points out, "Students need to see school
as valuable in terms that matter to them" (Jackson 2011a, 106). They want
to know how what they are learning today is going to be useful to their
lives outside of school.

Teachers have to keep this in mind when crafting lessons. In order
to maintain student interest and motivation, teachers must teach for a
deeper understanding that will take students well beyond the classroom.
Consequently, we need to select teaching points that students can easily
acknowledge as relevant now and useful in the future (Quate & McDermott 2009, 46).

Start every lesson by stating the purpose of the learning, why students
will be learning it, and how learning it will help them achieve something
valuable. Students learn best when they can see a clear sense of purpose
to the learning. Tell students why the work will help them reach the lesson objective and how learning that objective benefits them beyond the
classroom.

Today's student wants to know what's in it for them. And we need to
provide that answer.

Motivating Students to See Learning As Valuable

We sometimes confuse convincing students to cooperate with motivating them. Motivating students to learn is more about inspiring them to
value education than it is about enticing them to participate in an activity.
Robyn Jackson establishes that "motivation isn't about compliance or
control; it's about choice. Rather than look for ways to compel or trick
students into doing what we ask, we can help them make the choice to
invest in the classroom" (Jackson 2011a, 18).

Motivation is not simply about creating fictitious "real world" problems to fit the curriculum; it is more about *how* learning impacts life every
day. Motivation comes about through engagement in authentic, real-life
learning topics related to issues or dilemmas in which students can play a
key role in making some difference.

Having enough class time is an issue, though. With the implementation
of the Common Core State Standards, teachers sense the pressure even

more. Learning can sometimes feel reduced to pleading with students to get motivated. It is tempting to cut out anything that may take time away from teaching to the test, often sacrificing opportune moments for growth. Lifelong learners want to participate in class, try hard, challenge themselves, and complete assignments because doing them is personally important to them, not because we tell them to—and certainly not because of a test that measures a one-day performance.

The truth is that all students are motivated—about something. It just may not be about school. They have decided somewhere along the way that education doesn't matter, it isn't for them, or they can't succeed—so why try. They choose not to invest. We need to strike when the iron is hot: celebrate small victories, notice what inspires students, and use it to our advantage. It can be as simple as projecting students into the learning by asking, "Suppose you were . . . what might you do? Why?" Or "How could you use this in your life?" And "Why do you need to learn this?" Appeal to emotions—learn what makes them tick, and infuse it in the language of the classroom.

Providing Choice

There is much evidence that when students are given more opportunity to participate in decisions about schoolwork, they miss school less, are more creative, and put in more time on task (Kohn 1993, 12). Students feel proud when they create something from a desire to do so. We cannot underestimate the power in that.

Choice is one of the ways to put students in control of their learning—to build their sense of autonomy, to ensure that they have a voice (Jensen 2006, 16). Students take ownership and feel more fully invested when they are given some choices during the day. Providing options deepens the neural connections necessary in creating a pathway to the learning.

To be honest, doesn't it just feel better when we choose to do something rather than being told we have to do it? Having choices brings a sense of freedom and empowerment. And isn't that what being a lifelong learner is all about?—choosing to learn.

Pink (2009) advises giving more choice in four areas: task, time, team, and technique.

- Task: Simply stated, when we allow students to do projects, reading, and research around their interests, they are more engaged. In fact, homework completion improves dramatically when we provide options, and students get more out of it. (See appendix D for a sample on providing choice in homework.)
- Time: It is important for students to learn how to manage their time when completing long-term projects. Have them decide how to spend their time in order to progress effectively through an assignment. Include the process of deciding how to manage time into the learning. Model how you navigate through a long-term project successfully. Provide plenty of opportunities for practice.
- Provide a chunk of time each day for students to choose a way to show mastery of the learning. This could be in centers, contracts, tic-tac-toe boards, or menu ideas. (See appendix D for a sample tic-tac-toe board.) You can make it more informal by simply providing several options for students to choose one or two they must complete during a given time slot. We call them "must-dos" and "can-dos."
- Team: Give students a choice sometimes whether they would like to work on a project or assignment alone, with a partner, or in a small group.
- Technique: Provide students with a variety of ways to show mastery of the learning. Would they prefer to write an essay, perform a skit, create a children's book, make trading cards, use a Prezi, Glogster, or design a 3-D model? The options are endless. When we give students choice on how they would like to show what they know, we give them opportunity to strengthen their strengths, to shine, and most importantly, to see themselves as valuable assets to the learning.

We want to mention how important it is, however, to be careful to match choices according to your learning goals, keeping the focus on purposeful learning, not simply supplying activities to keep students busy. The ideas for choice must come from your intended purpose for the lesson.

The power is not just in providing choice; it is in providing meaningful, purposeful choice around the objective of the learning. As Robyn Jackson attests, choice is worthwhile "as long as students can demonstrate how this work will move them toward attainment of one or more of the clearly defined learning objectives you provide" (Jackson 2011a, 48).

Living a Life That Values Learning

Ellin Keene challenges each of us to live our lives as intellectually curious leaders for our students and our colleagues (Keene 2008, 17).

Teachers that value learning see themselves as lifelong students. They are never quite content with what they know. They strive to improve for the good of their students and for the joy that comes from learning. They want to reinvent the wheel.

Carol Dweck states that "The great teachers believe in the growth of the intellect and talent, and they are fascinated with the process of learning" (Dweck 2006, 194). They are captivated with learning and find delight in discovering something new.

LIFELONG LEARNERS SEE LEARNING AS VALUABLE

> People are wise, not in proportion to their experience but in proportion to their capacity for experience.
>
> —George Bernard Shaw

There is a great satisfaction in learning for the sake of learning. When we grasp the idea that knowledge is valuable, we try hard to know more, to improve. We become teachable.

Lifelong learners understand the capacity of their own minds. They see experience and hard work as teachers. They welcome disequilibrium, because they know the benefit of wrestling through it. They use whatever comes their way as an opportunity to learn.

Lifelong learners appreciate what life has to offer and they strive to grow from it.

7

Lifelong Learners Are Collaborative

Coming together is a beginning, staying together is progress, and working together is success.

—Henry Ford

WHAT IS BEING COLLABORATIVE?

The Merriam-Webster definition of *collaborative* is "to work jointly with others or together especially in an intellectual endeavor; to participate or assist in a joint effort to accomplish an end."

Collaboration returns greater value than solo thinking and yields a higher return. It is characterized by positive goal interdependence with individual accountability. Collaboration is working together to accomplish shared goals. In collaborative situations, lifelong learners work toward outcomes that are beneficial to themselves and beneficial to all group members.

Students learn best when they have the opportunity to discuss ideas with their peers in a nose-to-nose and toes-to-toes interaction (Gregory & Parry 2006). Ellin Keene establishes that "when we engage in dialogue about ideas, we are creating new knowledge. The volley between two minds with mutual interest isn't limited to sharing the known; when people engage in discourse, they are inventing new meaning, new interpretation that add a layer to earlier ideas" (Keene 2008, 197).

This experience contrasts with traditional classroom strategies that often produce a competitive environment in which students are pitted against each other to attain a particular goal, usually a high grade that is granted to only a few students. To this end, the student works alone, aiming at a goal different from and often unrelated to the learning goals of other students.

WHY IS COLLABORATION IMPORTANT TO BECOMING A LIFELONG LEARNER?

Collaboration means pulling individual strengths together to accomplish a common goal. This "one for all and all for one" approach to life is an essential ingredient in order to succeed in today's global economy. In spite of that, our current educational system typically promotes individualism and independence. Yet, it is really a sense of interdependence that is vital to successful and satisfying functioning in the adult world.

From all sides of the globe, people recognize that survival depends upon our capacity for cooperation, interdependence, and respect for diversity. The classroom environment should really reflect what the future holds by re-creating the idea of a "journey we are taking together," not "student versus student" (Costa & Kallick 2009, 95).

According to Jeanne Gibbs, collaboration means

- Negotiation rather than hostility
- Cooperation, not just competition
- Sharing and conserving resources
- Community building through consensus
- People coming together to help one another do what few can do alone (Gibbs 2006, 24)

Students are more effective interpersonally as a result of working collaboratively than when they work alone. Lifelong learners with effective collaborative skills are more able to take the perspective of others, are more positive about taking part in controversy, have better developed interaction skills, and have a more positive expectation about working with others than students from competitive or individualistic settings (Johnson & Johnson 1999).

In preparation for the world beyond the classroom, students need to be provided with frequent opportunities to practice these collaborative techniques. By listening to different perspectives and dialoguing about them, we become more strategic and knowledgeable—the result being improved communication and collaboration with both peers and adults.

There are notable advantages inherent in collaborative learning that students may not encounter in traditional classroom settings. One of the most valuable uses of collaborative learning is to teach social and interpersonal skills. Collaboration affirms and values different cultures, experiences, and opinions. When students work collaboratively, they learn more, are more likely to transfer the learning, and have more positive thoughts about their learning situation that when they work in a more individualistic or competitive environment (Quate & McDermott 2009, 76),

WHAT COGNITIVE PROCESSES FOSTER COLLABORATION?

1. Interdependence

Interdependence refers to a sense that each team member's contribution is valuable and necessary in order to achieve goals. The first step to creating an atmosphere of positive interdependence is setting a mutual goal that is reachable only if all members of the team participate. The goal should be structured so that every team member is responsible for learning the material and ensuring that every other group member learns the material (Johnson & Johnson 1999).

Being accepted and valued by peers is an essential factor in building confidence and ownership of one's learning. Cooperative techniques allow students to practice with the interpersonal and interdependent behaviors they will need to use as lifelong learners.

It is important to differentiate between having students sit together, giving them freedom to talk, but working on their assignment individually, and creating groups that foster interdependence. The key is to provide one clear goal that requires each member of the group to be prepared to be accountable both as an individual and as a group member, and these groups need ongoing teacher guidance.

In an *individualistic* learning situation, students are independent of one another and are working toward a set criterion in which their success depends on strictly on their own performance.

In a *collaborative* classroom that fosters interdependence, students are actually invited to participate in setting very clear, specific goals that are embedded in the content being delivered. This ensures that various students' interests are addressed. The goal communicates that group members are in this together and need to be as concerned with other group members' understanding of the material as they are with their own. The team members can then share their own knowledge and ways in which they learn. This is done in a respectful environment that focuses on higher-level thinking skills. By actively listening to the opinions of others and being willing to participate in creative exchanges, students begin to think in a diverse and more critical manner.

Suppose, for example, the students have just read a chapter on colonial America and are required to prepare a product on the topic. While a more traditional teacher might ask all students to write a ten-page essay, the collaborative teacher might ask students to choose how they would like to show their understanding and form groups according to the students' choices. One group could plan a videotape; another could dramatize events in colonial America; others could investigate original sources that support or do not support the textbook chapter and draw comparisons among them; and some could write a research paper. The point here is twofold: in a collaborative setting, (1) students have opportunities to ask and investigate questions of personal interest, and (2) they have a voice in the decision-making process. These opportunities are essential for both self-regulated learning and motivation (Tinzmann et al. 1990, 17).

The idea of "success breeds success" is worthwhile as teachers create the criteria for group members. It's important to articulate the specific behaviors that students are expected to demonstrate in order to have clear models of collaboration. Be thoughtful about group membership (ideally, three or four persons).

A word of caution here: be sensitive to students with high absentee rates. Distribute those students with high absentee rates evenly among the groups to make sure there are no groups with more than one. "The group membership must be stable enough for the group to be productive" (Quate & McDermott 2009).

Two of Our Favorite Ideas for Empowering Students to Increase Interdependence

Jigsaw
- Arrange students in home groups (three to four students usually work best). Students number off.
- Ahead of time, create an activity or experiment that is chunked into numbered parts, or find a piece of text related to the lesson purpose and chunk it into as many parts as you have assigned group members.
- Students leave their home groups and form expert groups according to their numbers. Expert groups will work on their chunk of the assignment or task.
- Create some type of advance organizer for expert groups to track their learning and thinking in order to share with their home group. The ideas are endless here. It really depends upon your goal for the lesson. (See appendix E for some examples in helping students track their thinking.)
- Students return to their home groups and are accountable for teaching what they learned as experts. (See appendix E for sample directions for students to use in a jigsaw.)

Paired Reading
1. Teacher creates a bookmark or poster of high-level comprehension questions to ask while doing paired reading.
2. Pairs can either share a picture book or each have a copy of the text.
3. If pairs each have a copy of text to be read, they should sit ear to ear facing in opposite directions. If they are sharing a picture book, they should sit shoulder to shoulder with the text between them.
4. One person reads aloud quietly a paragraph or two for an article or page of a textbook. If pairs are reading a picture book, have each student read a page.

5. The other person follows along in the reading and then asks a comprehension question about the selection to check for understanding. Both answer the question together.
6. Switch roles and continue.

WHAT DOES IT TAKE TO BE A COLLABORATIVE LEARNER?

Collaboration provides a positive structure for learning to occur. Having opportunities for dialogue motivates students to be active composers of meaning. Good collaborators are flexible, good communicators, and show empathy. To this end, it is important to keep in mind that the tools needed for successful collaborators do not simply "happen" by creating cooperative groups in our classrooms, but rather need modeling and practice so that they will become automatic.

Collaboration requires that students take more responsibility for their learning. For successful lifelong learners, collaboration becomes the natural approach to problem solving and includes a focus on placing what is best for the team before self, and on learning how to bring out the best thinking in their teammates. Each new situation brings the opportunity to demonstrate flexibility, as well as empathy.

There is evidence that some essential factors are present in successful learning experiences, and good collaboration skills are a key ingredient to becoming a lifelong learner.

Students who learn good collaboration skills

1. Grow in social and emotional competency
2. Achieve greater academic performance
3. Communicate and work well with others
4. Value diverse abilities and cultural differences
5. Assume responsibility for their own behavior
6. Develop critical thinking and collaborative skills
7. Improve their sense of self-worth and mastery of academics (Gibbs 2006)

ACCOUNTABILITY FOR LEARNING

If students are not accountable for their own learning, there's a good chance that some of them will become social loafers (Johnson & Johnson 1999). "Social loafing" refers to students not carrying their weight and relying on group members to complete their work—not contributing, not doing their fair share. Call it what it is. This validates the problem and doesn't single any one person out. If you notice a few "social loafers," you may just want to stop the activity and state that social loafers rely on the rest of the group to do the work and are slacking off and for your students to make sure they are not being a social loafer. Ask the students to stop for a minute and reflect on their own behavior in the group so far, and rate themselves on the "social loafing" scale, and explain their rating (Johnson & Johnson 1999).

Business leaders say that more jobs are lost among American workers due to the inability to work well with others than due to a lack of knowledge. Daniel Pink states that an important twenty-first-century skill is the ability to work with others—whether we like them or not and whether we agree with them or not. The last century was about information; this century will be about skills (Pink 2005). As much as we would like to think that we know it all, we don't. We will need to know how to collaborate to get a job done well.

Students need to assess their own contributions to both the work and their collaborative efforts. Groups should do the same, and they should create action plans for ongoing improvement. This must be put in place before, during, and after whatever assignment the group is working on.

It is important to have students assess the social objectives as well as the content objectives of the lesson. This not only transfers teachers' responsibility but internalizes both the social and content learning. Jeanne Gibbs highlights that when students become responsible to each other, accountability for performance and behavior is shared by the students and the teacher. The wall between teacher and students melts away (Gibbs 2006, 52).

Have student groups develop agreements for how they will work together. Give examples of how to do this, allowing students time to reflect on an occasion when they worked in a group that was particularly effective. Have them remember a time when group work was a disaster (no names included). Based on the discussion, have students generate a list of three to five agreements that will define how the group will work effectively together. Then brainstorm ways to solve problems based on the role-playing scenario of the "bad group." Post the solution ideas so that students can refer to it during a time of need. Every once in a while, you can refer to the poster and ask the students to quietly reflect on "how well you are holding up your end of the bargain."

Group members can also brainstorm ways to get them started such as, "Where did we leave off yesterday?" Have the group make a poster of possible things to say or do. Collaborative skills don't just happen on their own. Successful collaborative skills must be explicitly taught.

In truly collaborative settings, the following skills are key to fostering both active learning and individual accountability:

1. Engage students in identifying the need for the skill (role-play, stories, brainstorm, inquiry)
2. Model the skill (looks like/sounds like/feels like)
3. Practice, practice, practice, with self-assessment on how well it is being used
4. Provide frequent, effective teacher feedback
5. Remind students to use the skill independently
6. Pose reflective questions on individual accountability and interdependence
7. Celebrate consistent use of the skill

When planning an active learning task, answering the following questions ahead of time will help you clarify your goals and structure:

- What are your objectives for the activity?
- What lifelong qualities would you like reinforced in the collaboration?
- Who is interacting? Will students pair up with someone beside them? Or perhaps with someone sitting behind or in front of them? Should they pair up with someone with a different background? Someone they don't know yet?

- When does the activity occur during the class? Beginning? Middle? End? How much time are you willing to spend on it?
- How will they show their understanding?
- How will they show individual accountability?
- Will they write down their answers/ideas/questions, draw them, or just discuss them?
- Will they turn in the responses or not?
- Will you grade their responses or not? How will you provide meaningful feedback?
- How will they share any paired work with the whole class? How will you use and share the feedback and insight you gained from their responses?
- If they are responding to a question you pose, how are you going to ensure that they leave with confidence in their understanding?
- What preparation do you need to use the activity? What background knowledge do the students need in order to participate fully? (Johnson & Johnson 1999)

Two of Our Favorite Ideas for Empowering Students to Increase Accountability

Numbered Heads Together This page has been copied with permission from Kagan Publishing & Professional Publishing, 2009, 1(800)933-2667. http://www.KaganOnline.com.

USE: Classbuilding, Higher-Level Thinking, Mastery, Determining Importance, Summarizing and Synthesizing the Learning, Reflecting

PURPOSE: All students are engaged while reviewing a concept, answering higher-level questions, determining importance, summarizing and synthesizing the learning, debriefing, developing vocabulary, and learning more about each other.

DIRECTIONS:

1. Students form groups of three or four and number off.
2. Teacher poses question.
3. Students think and write in silence.
4. Teacher calls a huddle and students put their heads together to confer.

5. Teacher calls a number and students with that number share their answers. Students can go up to the board, use mini white erase boards, or simply call out chorally.
6. Repeat steps 1–5 until all questions are answered.

4-2-1   4—Start with a group of four. In that group, students work on a problem-solving activity or some kind of challenging task. Warn students that they will individually produce their own work at the end of the class. Provide ample time for good collaboration.

2—When the time is up, the groups of four split up, and each person finds one other person from a different group to work with. This new pair continues the work on the task for a specified amount of time or works on a similar problem. Allow for time for effective collaboration.

1—At the end of the time, students reflect individually to produce their own task (Quate & McDermott 2009, 78).

Collaborative learning encourages both individual accountability and interpersonal relationships. Anxiety levels go down, while content retention and interpersonal skills go up. When group members share jobs, there is provision for individual accountability. Assessment can be given to individuals as well as to a group to ensure that each person has mastered the required learning. Because the focus on interpersonal skills is a priority, all of those components—encouragement, consensus building, good communication—are carefully addressed in the design of the task.

PROMOTING POSITIVE INTERACTION

When members of a group help one another, share information, and take time to listen, achievement levels go up, material is remembered longer, and students move beyond surface learning. Students working cooperatively tend to like each other better.

Students in cooperative learning situations also show increased self-esteem, self-efficacy, and confidence in the future. They tend to have a higher regard for school, for the subject they are studying, and for their teachers.

Two of Our Favorite Ideas for Empowering
Students to Promote Positive Interaction

Carousel Brainstorming

1. Before the lesson—determine the size of the groups (3–5 works well) and how the groups will be established. Create questions, quotes, or statements that have potential for rich conversation and critical thinking. Include a different one for each group and write it on chart paper.

2. Form groups and give each group a different-color marker to use and the chart paper with the given prompt.

3. Students will read the prompt and brainstorm possible responses, writing down on a piece of loose-leaf paper as many ideas as time allows. Come to a consensus on how to synthesize the ideas from the brainstorming. Assign a scribe to write the response on the chart paper. Try not to give too much time at each circuit, so that the remaining groups have something to contribute.

4. Direct students to stop writing, bring their marker, and move clockwise to the next prompt. Now students are expected to read the prompt and the previous group's response. Students should piggyback ideas as they too brainstorm and synthesize.

5. Continue clockwise steps 3 and 4.

6. Students revisit the charts in a gallery-walk style.

7. Collect the chart paper. Students return to their original groups and begin reading the intended text silently while annotating and responding in the margins. Partners are formed within the groups to compare and contrast annotations.

8. Post responses from the brainstorming. Provide each group with a different color sticky note and challenge them to add to or revise their original responses, include a question, or make a connection. Add sticky notes to each chart and reflect on the learning (Daniels & Steineke 2011, 122–23; Beers 2003; Wilhelm 2002).

Appointment Clock This is a very popular and easy way to form groups for upper elementary, middle school, and high school students.

- Print a clock face. Draw several arrows around the circumference of the clock indicating certain "times." (See reproducible in appendix E of a sample clock face to copy for Clock Partners.)
- The students "travel" around the room and ask another student to be their one o'clock partner. Both students write their names under the corresponding numbers on both their clocks. They then find two o'clock partners, three o'clock partners, and so on until all the clocks have been filled out.
- We always specify that students can list a particular individual's name only once. According to the makeup of the class, we may insist that the student choose an equal number of boys and girls.
- It is a good idea to collect the clocks as soon as they are filled before handing them back to the students. (This helps if someone loses one.)
- As group tasks arise, tell the students to find, for example, their two o'clock appointment.
- Students will then know who their partner will be for that assignment.
- We found clock partners to be comforting for shy or more socially awkward students because they don't have to rely on being chosen.

HOW CAN I BECOME A TEACHER WHO PROMOTES COLLABORATION IN MY PRACTICE?

We could learn a lot from crayons: some are sharp, some are pretty, some are dull, while others are bright, some have weird names, but we have to learn to live in the same box.

—Anonymous

Cooperative learning is not impromptu but is well planned and well managed, and student tasks need to challenge groups by requiring committed effort on the part of all members. Happy, well-functioning groups matched with appropriate tasks and given adequate time constraints run smoothly.

Planning needs to be organized, with all materials carefully prepared and sorted prior to the class. Teacher responsibility includes ongoing monitoring and effective feedback for all students. Just as lesson planning needs to be segmented to ensure time for teacher talk, student talk, and formative assessment, learning groups will need to respond to specific prompts to demonstrate both group and individual responsibility.

To guide and strengthen students' growth as collaborators, teachers should be ready to

- Give prompt and meaningful feedback
- Assess student development and use of the qualities of a lifelong learner
- Clarify directions
- Recognize and celebrate hard work
- Encourage higher-level thinking skills such as analysis, application, evaluation, and synthesis
- Affirm positive interaction and effort
- Informally assess student learning and collaboration
- Celebrate success
- Reflect on both the content and the collaborative process

It is critical to provide time to reflect after group activities. Challenge students to evaluate their interactions. This can be used as an "exit ticket" or journal as a way to self-assess effective collaboration skills.

Some ideas for questions

- How do you feel about the work your group did today? Why?
- What role did you play in the group's ability to collaborate?
- What can you celebrate about it? What would you do to improve?
- What could your team do to improve the way you get along and/or work together?
- What is your favorite thing about being on this team?
- What is hard about working in groups? What can you do to change that?
- What can I do, as your teacher, to support you in your efforts to collaborate?
- What qualities of a lifelong learner did you employ while working in your groups today? How did using that quality help you?

Always look for different ways to embed collaborative opportunities in your instructional delivery. After modeling or explaining a concept, stop and have groups summarize or describe the concept. For skill reinforcement, groups can convene to practice, memorize, or review for an assessment. Even homework checks can be enhanced by group review for accuracy.

Johnson & Johnson summarized more than six hundred studies reporting the significant benefits of learning through cooperation:

1. Greater productivity and academic achievement
2. Constructive thinking skills: planning, inferring, analyzing, gathering data, and strategizing
3. Social competency: trust in others, perspective taking, sense of personal identity, awareness of interdependence, sense of direction and purpose
4. Motivation: high expectations of success and achievement; high commitment and persistence
5. Social support: constructive management of stress; high-quality relationships that extend life and help people recover from illness
6. Psychological health: the ability to develop, maintain and improve one's relationships and situation in life; success in achieving goals
7. Self-esteem improved due to positive peer relations and to improved academic achievement (Johnson & Johnson 1999)

We have included a few simple but very effective starting points for shifting from a traditional teacher-centered classroom to one that promotes collaboration and discourse:

- Arrange desks so that students can easily talk and listen to each other.
- Encourage students to generate questions and to direct their questions to the rest of the class, not simply to the teacher.
- Promote and maintain an atmosphere of acceptance. When students feel safe, they are more willing to take risks.
- Do not always stand in the front of the room. The simple act of standing in various spots in the room with redirect the conversation from a teacher-student discourse to a student-centered discussion.
- When in doubt, remain silent. Give students a chance to wrestle with the learning.
- Stop and write. Allow brief writing moments to promote deep thinking and meaningful conversations.

- Prepare high-level questions ahead of time to springboard the conversation.
- Allow think time before the conversation begins.
- Train students to recognize when they are getting off track and encourage them to support each other when it happens. Model how to prompt someone back to understanding.
- When students ask questions, try not to answer right away. Redirect questions back to the students by asking follow-up questions.

LIFELONG LEARNERS ARE COLLABORATIVE

In the long history of humankind (and animal kind, too) those who learned to collaborate and improvise most effectively have prevailed.

—Charles Darwin

Lifelong learners understand that working toward shared goals is beneficial to us as individuals and to all members of the collaborative group. The research is clear: collaboration improves our attempts to succeed.

Working collaboratively provides ways to develop respect for ourselves and others. Lifelong learners build interpersonal communication skills that make them good citizens with increased confidence in the future, resulting in better opportunities for success.

Conclusion

We need to keep teaching on the frontiers of our thinking. Our work will always bear the label, "To Be Continued . . ."

—Shelly Harwayne (1992, 338)

It is hard to believe we are at the end of this book. This journey began fifteen years ago with a passion to understand exactly what qualities lifelong learners enjoy. We weren't looking for ideals—more grandiose words to post on a mission statement; we were searching for ways to take the challenge down from the walls and make lifelong learning a real possibility for *all* students. Our purpose was then and is now is to help students reach their highest potential, and we hope this book will play some part in that.

What is presently set before us is a challenge to live out these qualities as an inspiration and a message that lifelong learning is continuous. This voyage is not finished just because we understand what it takes to become a lifelong learner. Lifelong learning is exactly what it says: learning that is alive, constant, and life changing.

We need to live out the qualities boldly for ourselves and our students:

- *Be tenacious*: Real change takes time. It will take a few years to infuse the qualities successfully. Don't try to apply everything all at once. Remember it literally took us a decade to try everything in this book and feel good about it. Be patient with yourself. Just commit to stay in the game.

- *Be reflective*: Use reflection in your daily life, both professionally and personally. There is a lesson to be learned in every life experience. We just need to stay open to it. If writing helps you reflect, keep a journal. Set aside time each day for silence. Moments of quiet reflection often bring clarity, even in the midst of what may seem like an impossible situation.

- *Be metacognitive:* Metacognition means thinking about our thinking. The first step to being truly metacognitive is to shift your thinking. Ellin Keene challenges us to "propel our teaching forward, from good to great, from effective to artistic. We must do what may be hardest of all—rethink what we believe is already working" (Keene 2008, 57).

- *Be a divergent thinker*: Be daring enough to expand your horizons. Read on different subjects, discover new places, and spend time with people very different from you. To stimulate divergent thinking, you need to take your own first steps toward living outside of your comfort zone. You can feed creativity with the willingness to take risks and try new things.

- *Be self-efficacious*: We can dismiss the idea that IQ is fixed in stone. We can now pinpoint how we "grow" our intelligence. It takes hard work, confidence, and tenacity, but it is possible. Resting on that fact alone will increase our sense of self-efficacy.

  We have control over where our learning brings us. There is both freedom and responsibility in knowing that we can develop our intellect with hard work. Chuck Yeager, the real-life hero of *The Right Stuff*, attested to this when he said, "There is no such thing as a natural-born pilot. Whatever my aptitude or talents, becoming a proficient pilot was hard work, really a lifetime's learning experience. . . . The best pilots fly more than the others, that's why they're the best" (Dweck 2006, 32).

- *Be someone who sees learning as valuable*: Pericone (2005) asserts that students may not learn any of the content of your class, but one thing they are always learning is who you are. We must model what it means to approach learning with enthusiasm. Students will not buy into the idea that learning is valuable if they don't see it being lived out in our teaching practice. We need to openly display passion and joy as we pursue learning.

- *Be collaborative*: It is helpful to enlist an accountability partner or two as you begin to incorporate the qualities in your practice. Working together professionally reaps more rewards for students—and truthfully, it's more fun that way. Helen Keller put it best when she said, "Alone we can do so little; together we can do so much."

While this marks the end of our time together, we hope that you will feel empowered and equipped with some new tools to continue your work in stretching and growing the possibilities within each of your students. We hope this book may be the one resource that remains ever in reach, always providing practical strategies and continual encouragement to your professional growth.

A lifelong learner is just that: a student who eagerly commits to continual growth and development. So, as you plan and deliver these activities for students, make sure that you too become the student. When you assess the progress of your students, remember to self-assess your own success. Are you reaching your potential as a lifelong learner?

We feel so blessed and honored to have shared this journey with you. We reflect on the paths that led us here, side-by-side on the road to empowering students to become lifelong learners. And we are grateful.

Tomorrow must find us expanding our knowledge and experience, not stagnating in the status quo. We must never be satisfied, never feel that the task is complete. Stimulating and encouraging learning in our students and in ourselves is our life's work. Today is the day to begin anew.

And so our journey continues . . .

Appendix A

Resources for Chapter 2:
"Lifelong Learners Are Reflective"

Name: _____

Summarizing and Synthesizing the Reading

Directions:

During Reading:

Read the assigned text silently. As you read, write down in the squares below one or two words that best summarize each section. Choose word(s) from the text or any word that you feel best describes the main idea of that section.

After Reading:

- Share your key words in a small group. If you hear a word that you think needs to be included above, add it to your list.
- If you had to advertise this article as a TV documentary, movie, or book, how would you do it? What words from the word bank above would be necessary to include? You may only choose five to ten words from the list.

- Now create a catchy title for your advertisement. Be creative. Remember that you are trying to get people to want to watch or read about your topic.

My Top 10 List

Name: _____   Date: _____

Topic: _____

Directions:

Reflect on what you learned. Create a "Top 10 List" on what you consider to be the most important ideas about the topic.

1	
2	
3	
4	
5	
6	
7	
8	
9	
10	

Self-Evaluation of Today's Learning Objective

Give out a self-evaluation exit ticket to each student.

Name _____   Date _____

Circle on the continuum below how clearly you understood

_____ *(place your learning objective here).*

Did not   Kind of know it   Could teach

understand at all   it tomorrow.

  1   **2**   **3**   **4**   **5**

Include your proof of mastery (examples, illustrations, explanation) or questions you still have:

Name _____   Date _____

Circle on the continuum below how clearly you understood

_____ *(place your learning objective here).*

Did not   Kind of know it   Could teach

understand at all   it tomorrow.

  1   **2**   **3**   **4**   **5**

Include your proof of mastery (examples, illustrations, explanation) or questions you still have:

Self-Evaluation of the Student's
Effort toward Learning Today's Objective

Give out a self-evaluation of student effort toward intended learning goals handout to each student.

Name of student _____   Date _____

Circle on the continuum below what best represents how well you succeeded in meeting your

learning goals today.

Did not   Met all my

do my best   learning goals.

| 1 | 2 | 3 | 4 | 5 |

Here is what I accomplished:

_____

_____

_____

Here is my plan for tomorrow:

_____

_____

(Hollas 2005, 143)

Self-Evaluation of the Student's Use of the Qualities of a Lifelong Learner

Name: _____   Date: _____

How much did I use the qualities it takes to be a lifelong learner today?

QUALITIES	NEVER	SOMETIMES	MOSTLY	EXPLANATION
Tenacious				
Reflective				
Metacognitive				
Divergent Thinker				
Efficacious				
See Learning as Valuable				
Collaborative				

- What quality do I find easy to practice? Give a few examples of how you show it.

- What quality do I have difficulty practicing? What can I do to change that tomorrow?

- Choose one quality you will focus on for a week and share how you will purposely use it to make a difference in your life and in the life of others.

Leftovers Again?

Name: _____

Directions:

Step 1: Go back and reflect on your notes from the reading. If what you learned instantly turned into a plate of leftovers, what part of your learning would you consider to be the main dish (the most important idea in the reading)? Explain your reasoning.

TODAY'S MAIN DISH – (Explain your reasoning)

Step 2: Go back and reflect on your notes from the reading. If what you learned instantly turned into a plate of leftovers, what part of your learning would you consider to be two side dishes (details that support the main idea)? Explain your reasoning

TODAY'S SIDE DISH #1 – (Explain your reasoning)

TODAY'S SIDE DISH #2 – (Explain your reasoning)

Step 3: Go back and reflect on your notes from the reading. If what you learned instantly turned into a plate of leftovers, what part of your learning would you consider to be the dessert (interesting, but maybe not key to the learning, draws upon emotions, etc.)? Explain your reasoning.

TODAY'S DESSERT – (Explain your reasoning)

Source: Pearse & Walton (2011, 174).

Appendix B

Resources for Chapter 3:
"Lifelong Learners Are Metacognitive"

Directions: Place six strips of highlighter tape in each column.

Table B.1

METACOGNITION AND THE 24-HOUR PRINCIPLE: ACTIVE READING CARD		
Determining Importance (VIPs)	*Making Connections Reactions/Responses*	*Questioning*

METACOGNITION AND THE 24-HOUR PRINCIPLE: ACTIVE READING CARD		
Determining Importance (VIPs)	*Making Connections Reactions/Responses*	*Questioning*

Name: _____   **READER'S NOTEBOOK**

Metacognition and the 24-Hour Principle

1. Actively read your text using the active reading card.
2. As you read, determine very important points (VIPs). A good strategy is to read a page and ask yourself what important points did you read on that page, and then flag it or them with the highlighter tape as a VIP.
3. Make connections as you read by asking: What does what I'm reading remind me of? Something else you learned? Something in your life?
4. What questions come to mind as you read? Flag them with your highlighter tape.
5. Before twenty-four hours have passed, revisit your VIPs, connections, and questions and *record them on the following graphic organizer*. If you answered your initial question(s), include the answer(s) as well. Circle any unanswered questions to bring to class.
6. Include your insights and reflections on each page as you reread your notes.

Name: _____   **READER'S NOTEBOOK**

Figure B.2

Determining Importance Include Very Important Points + the page number where your VIP is found VIPs & page #s	Making Connections Connections I made either to my life or something else I read or learned	Questioning Questions that came to mind while I read and answers if I found them.

Insights and Reflections—What insights or reflections do you have from the ideas on this page?

_____

Give-One-Get-One

Directions:

1. Using your brainstorming list, decide on your favorite three ideas and jot them down in the first row of your Give-One-Get-One hand-out.
2. Get up, mosey around the room a bit, and find a partner and freeze.
3. *GIVE ONE* idea from your list to your partner. Share why it is important to you.
4. *GET ONE* idea for your list from your partner and listen to why that response is important.
5. Move to a new partner and repeat the process until your blocks are full or until time is up.

If your list and your partner's list are identical, you must brainstorm together another example of exemplary design for learning that can be added to both of your lists.

Give-One-Get-One Handout

Name: _____

Figure B.3

GIVE: Put one of your top three ideas here to give away.	GIVE: Put one of your top three ideas here to give away	GIVE: Put one of your top three ideas here to give away
GET:	GET:	GET:
GET:	GET:	GET:
GET:	GET:	GET:

Appendix B

Name: _____ Date: _____

Exploring Metacognition (Thinking about My Thinking)
Double-Entry Reader Response Journal (Template)

(Shared with permission from Stephanie Pierce)

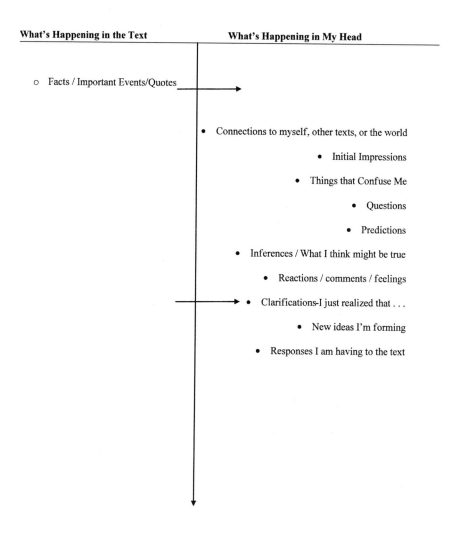

What's Happening in the Text

o Facts / Important Events/Quotes

What's Happening in My Head

- Connections to myself, other texts, or the world
  - Initial Impressions
  - Things that Confuse Me
  - Questions
  - Predictions
- Inferences / What I think might be true
  - Reactions / comments / feelings
- Clarifications-I just realized that . . .
  - New ideas I'm forming
- Responses I am having to the text

Name: _____   Date: _____

Exploring Metacognition (Thinking about My Thinking)
Double-Entry Reader Response Journal

What's Happening in the Text	What's Happening in My Head

Understanding Question-Answer Relationships (QAR)

Table B.4

Right There Questions

The answer can be found in the text, can be easy to find, and is important. Normally the words in the question and the words in the answer can be found in the same sentence in the reading selection.

These questions usually result in one-word or short-phrase responses, and there is usually only one right answer.

This type of question may begin with: "Who is . . . ," "Where is . . . ," "What is . . . ," "When is . . . ," "How many . . . ," "When did . . . ," "Name . . . ," "What kind of . . ."

Think and Search Questions

The answer is in the selection, but you need to put together different pieces of information to find it. The answer comes from different places in the selection.

You will need to look back at the passage, find the information that the question refers to, and then think about how the information or ideas fit together.

"Think and Search" questions sometimes include the words, "The main idea of the passage is . . . ," "What caused . . . ," "Compare/contrast . . . ," "Summarize . . ."

Author and You Questions

The answer can NOT be found in the reading selection. You need to connect what you know about the world with what the author has written to answer this type of question.

This type of question could explain the theme of the story or how the author feels about specific topics.

Author and Me questions may begin with: "What is the author saying about . . . ," "How does the author feel about . . . ," "The passage suggests . . . ," "The speaker's attitude is . . . ," "The author implies . . ."

On My Own Questions

The answer can NOT be found in the reading selection, and you do not have to have read the story to figure out the answer. However, the question and answer are related to the reading selection in some way, usually in the form of personal opinion or previous knowledge about a subject.

"On My Own" questions sometimes include the words, "In your opinion . . . ," "Based on your experience . . . ," "Think about someone/something you know . . ."

This type of question may begin with: "How do you feel about . . . ," "Recall a time when you . . . ," "In your opinion . . . ," "Based on your experience . . ."

Thick Questions

Think and Search

Why do you think...?, What if?, How would you
feel if..?, What might....?

(Beth Newinghams, *Scholastic.com,* accessed April 9, 2013, http://hil.troy
.k12.mi.us/staff/bnewingham/myweb3/Frames%20thick.htm)

Thin Questions

Right There

When? Where? Who? How many?

(Beth Newinghams, *Scholastic.com,* accessed April 9, 2013, http://hill
.troy.k12.mi.us/staff/bnewingham/myweb3/PDF%20Files/Thick%20
Question%20Poster.pdf)

Before, During, and After (BDA) Question Prompts

BEFORE the learning/reading questions:

- What story clues are in the titles and pictures?
- Is this story real or make-believe? What makes you say that?
- Why do you want to read this story?
- If this story is real, what do you think you will learn? What makes you say that?
- How do you picture the setting? What makes you say that?
- What genre of writing does this text represent? Fiction? Nonfiction? Poetry? What makes you say that?
- Based on the genre of writing, how will you read this selection?
- What expectations do you have when you read nonfiction? Fiction? Poetry? What makes you say that?
- What do you already know about . . . ?
- What will the main character need or want? What makes you say that?
- What information could be researched to deepen your understanding of the text?
- Why are you reading this? What is your goal? (Set a purpose for reading.)
- What information do you hope this text will include?
- What questions do you hope this text will answer?
- Do you know this author's work? Have you read other pieces written by this author? What do you know about the kinds of writing this author has composed?
- Why do you think the author wrote this story or text?
- When you scan the text features (title, subtitle, headings, illustrations, captions, bold print, italicized phrases), what details can you collect to help you prepare for reading?
- Using the text structure, what do you think you will be learning about today? What makes you say that? What do you remember about . . . ?
- What do you think the title means?
- What does the title remind you of?
- What do you remember about . . . ? (Use the title of the lesson or text to prompt the thinking.)
- What is this similar to? What makes you say that?

- How is . . . the same as yesterday's story/text/lesson? How is it different?
- What do you notice about . . . ?
- How might you picture that? Explain.
- Why do you think . . . ?
- How might you categorize . . . ? Defend your choices.
- What do you predict will be the most important information in this passage? Why?

DURING the learning/reading questions:

- What will happen next in the story? What makes you say that?
- What do you understand from the paragraph you just read?
- Could you summarize its key ideas?
- How do you feel about the main character? Why do you feel that way?
- Why does the character act a certain way?
- Does the story or text make sense? Why? Why not?
- How will the story most likely end? What evidence leads you to believe that?
- How does the story or text remind you of your life? How is it different?
- What do you understand from what you just read?
- What picture is the author painting in your head?
- Do you need to reread so that you understand?
- Did the author make the story believable? Why or why not?
- What captivates you about the story/character/problem? Explain.
- Do you need to reread the paragraph to understand what the author is saying?
- Do you need to slow down your reading in order to understand the ideas? What strategies can you use to unlock the meanings in this text?
- What images can you visualize in order to build your understanding?
- What do you predict will happen next? What makes you say that?
- What are you surprised about? Why are you surprised?
- What do you have questions about? Where might you find those answers?

- Why didn't the character . . . ?
- What do you imagine the character to be like? What makes you say that?
- Have you read anything similar? Explain the similarities and differences.
- How is this different from what you expected to happen? How is it the same?
- How has your thinking changed? What caused your thinking to change?
- What phrase/word/image do you particularly like? Why?
- What does this reminds you of? Explain.
- What is difficult about being the character? Why is it difficult? What might make it easier? Why do you say that?
- What is interesting about the character/setting/theme? Why is that interesting to you?
- Would you want to be the character? Why? Why not?
- Would you want to be the character's friend? Why? Why not?
- What do you imagine the town/setting/place/house to be like? What makes you say that?
- Would you want to live in this story? Why? Why not?
- What about this story makes you angry, sad, etc.?
- Why did the story turn in that direction, or why did the author choose to shape it that way?
- What questions might you still have about . . . ?
- How is . . . the same as yesterday's lesson? How is it different?
- What can you add to that thought?
- What do you notice about . . . ?
- How might you picture that? Explain.
- Can you show me a part of the text where you have a question? What were you wondering when you read this part?
- Can you show me a part where you were confused? What was confusing about it?

AFTER the learning/reading questions:

- How did the story or text make you feel? What in the story made you feel that way?

- Which of your prereading predictions were confirmed?
- What do you like or dislike about the story? Explain.
- Which predictions were revised?
- What is the theme? How do you know?
- Who do you think would like the story? Why?
- Who would not like the story? Why?
- What are the main ideas of the story? How do you know this?
- How did your feelings about the character changed? What made them change?
- How are the character's actions and feelings different than they were at the beginning of the story? What made them change?
- What is the author trying to teach you? What makes you say that?
- What generalizations can be made using the details from the text?
- How did you feel about . . . ?
- What conclusions can you make from the details described in the selection?
- What cause-and-effect relationships were revealed?
- How did the author reveal descriptive information?
- What is the overall theme of this text?
- What connections did you make with the information in this text?
- Would you recommend this text to other readers? Why or why not?
- Can you show me a part where you were confused? What was confusing about it? What did you do to repair your understanding?
- At what point did you get off track? What did you do about it?
- What questions might you still have about . . . ?
- How is . . . the same as yesterday's lesson? How is it different?
- What do you notice about . . . ?
- What is the most important information in this passage?
- In your own words, this is about . . . ?
- From today's lesson, what might you be learning about tomorrow? What makes you say that?
- How is what you read about important in real life? Explain.
- What can you infer from . . . ? How did you make that inference?
- Where would you see this in real life? Explain.
- Can you make a generalization? Explain.
- How might you explain what you learned about that to a little child?
- How did your thinking change? Explain.

- What do you now understand about . . . that you didn't understand before?
- How do you know you know?
- How do you know you don't know?
- What do you see that is new to you? Provide clear and vivid examples.
- How is this similar to . . . ? How is it different?
- How would you describe the most important idea you learned today in one sentence?
- What was the main point of the lesson? What makes you say that?
- What are some new questions you generated from what you did in class today?
- What is something you would like me to know about your learning today?

The Geometry of Polygons—Creating Your Own Logo!
Fourth Quarter Performance Assessment

- Standard 2.9.8.H—Use simple geometric figures (e.g., triangles, squares, etc.) to create, through rotations, reflections, and translations.
- Standard 2.9.8.K—Analyze objects to determine whether they illustrate symmetry.

In this project, you will create a logo for yourself, your class, your favorite team, or any group you belong to (as long as it is school appropriate).

Rough Draft Requirements and Grade Defense

- You must create a logo on graph paper that includes at least two examples of each of the following: rotation, reflection, and translation. This will be your blueprint (rough draft).
- Each of the above transformations must be clearly visible and labeled in your blueprint, and you must be able to show them to me and defend how you know they are the designated transformations. Coordinates of preimage and image must be included and accurate.
- Your logo must include at least three different polygons. Before you come to your appointment to final draft (grade defense conference), you must be able to explain the definitions of each polygon.
- Your logo must show symmetry, and you must be able to explain the concept of symmetry. Coordinates of preimage and image must be included and accurate.
- Sign up for an appointment with me (using the appointment calendar) when you feel your blueprint is ready to move to final draft and showcase level. Bring your blueprint with you and complete your part of the grade defense rubric. Make sure you are able to defend each of the grades and the concepts required within them.
- You will not move to final piece until this part is perfect and ready to go. Therefore, do not make an appointment with me until you are sure you have met all the geometric requirements.

Final Draft Requirements (after grade defense conference)

- Your logo must be colored and neat.
- Your logo must be original and creative.
- Your logo must be an exact final draft, after all revisions, of your original blueprint.
- Your final draft must be matted and ready for showcase level.

Grading Rubric—Grade Defense—Rough Draft—Appointment necessary

Table B.5

Requirement	Possible Points	What score do you give yourself? Why?	What do I think? Why?
Present three polygons with a clear understanding of the concepts.	3 – CLEARLY EVIDENT: All polygons present and labeled with a thorough explanation of each concept. 2 – SOME EVIDENCE: Two polygons evident with a thorough explanation, or all three evident without a solid defense. 1 – LITTLE EVIDENCE: Not a clear understanding of the concepts and not all polygons present.		
Two translations evident with a clear understanding of the concept.	3 – CLEARLY EVIDENT: Translations present and labeled with a thorough explanation of concept. Coordinates or pre-image and image are included and accurate. 2 – SOME EVIDENCE: One piece missing from above. 1 – LITTLE EVIDENCE: Two pieces missing from above.		

Requirement	Possible Points	What score do you give yourself? Why?	What do I think? Why?
Two rotations evident with a clear understanding of the concept.	3 – CLEARLY EVIDENT: Rotations present and labeled with a thorough explanation of concept. Coordinates or pre-image and image are included and accurate. 2 – SOME EVIDENCE: One piece missing from above. 1 – LITTLE EVIDENCE: Two pieces missing from above.		
Two reflections evident with a clear understanding of the concept.	3 – CLEARLY EVIDENT: Reflections present and labeled with a thorough explanation of concept. Coordinates or pre-image and image are included and accurate. 2 – SOME EVIDENCE: One piece missing from above. 1 – LITTLE EVIDENCE: Two pieces missing from above.		
Symmetry is clearly labeled and accurate. Explanation is thorough.	3 – CLEARLY EVIDENT: Symmetry present and labeled with a thorough explanation of concept. Coordinates or pre-image and image are included and accurate. 2 – SOME EVIDENCE: One piece missing from above. 1 – LITTLE EVIDENCE: Two pieces missing from above.		
TOTAL:	15		

Grading Rubric—Final Draft—You may only begin this after your grade defense conference is approved.

Table B.6

Requirement	Possible Points	Points You Earned. Teacher Comment.
Creative	3 – STRONG EVIDENCE 2 – SOME EVIDENCE 1 – LITTLE EVIDENCE	
Neat	3 – STRONG EVIDENCE 2 – SOME EVIDENCE 1 – LITTLE EVIDENCE	
Colorful	3 – STRONG EVIDENCE 2 – SOME EVIDENCE 1 – LITTLE EVIDENCE	
Original	3 – STRONG EVIDENCE 2 – SOME EVIDENCE 1 – LITTLE EVIDENCE	
Matted	3 – MATTED 0 – NOT MATTED	
TOTAL:	15	

Rough Draft and Grade Defense (15 possible points) _____
Final Draft (15 possible points)_____
Total Grade for This Project_____

Name: _____

Speed Dating through Metacognition

Today you have the opportunity to read one of the best articles out there on teaching and learning. Then you are going to summarize and synthesize the reading by creating a character that would best represent the reading. You will need to become this character. The class will then experience "speed dating" through the other "characters" in the class.

Directions:

Follow the BDA reading tool below to help you become more metacognitive as you read.

Before Reading: THIEVES

Determining importance. Sometimes there is a lot of information on a page and not all of it is important. If you know where to look to find what's important, it will help you figure out how to make good predictions, and *predictions keep you involved as a reader.*

This prediction strategy is called THIEVES, and if you really use it, you will become smarter—guaranteed!

Before you begin the strategy, think about what thieves do. They break into a home really quickly and take whatever is important. Well, you are going to do a similar activity with reading. I want you to use the following text structures to make a prediction about what you think the most important ideas in your reading will be.

Using the THIEVES acronym, glance at each of the following text structures that are common in informational text. From this, make a prediction about what you think this reading will mainly be about. Write your prediction on the next page.

What do you predict will be the most important ideas in the reading?

_____

_____

_____

_____

_____

T.H.I.E.V.E.S.

T........ TITLE

What is the title?

What do I already know about this topic?

What does this topic have to do with the preceding lesson or chapter?

What do I think I will be reading about?

H.......HEADINGS/SUBHEADINGS

What does this heading tell me I will be reading about?

What is the topic of the paragraph beneath it?

How can I turn this heading into a question that is likely to be answered in the text?

I.......INTRODUCTION

Is there an opening paragraph, perhaps italicized?

Does the first paragraph introduce the chapter?

What does the introduction tell me I will be reading about?

E.......EVERY FIRST SENTENCE IN A PARAGRAPH

What do I think this article is going to be about, based on the first sentence in each paragraph?

V ....VISUALS AND VOCABULARY

Does the chapter include photographs, drawings, maps, charts, or graphs?

What can I learn from the visuals in a chapter?

How do captions help me better understand the meaning?

Is there a list of key vocabulary terms and definitions?

Are there important words in boldface type throughout the chapter?

Do I know what the bold-faced words mean?

Can I tell the meaning of the boldfaced words from the sentences in which they are embedded?

E.......END-OF-TEXT QUESTIONS

What do the questions ask?

What information do I learn from the questions?

S.......SUMMARY

What do I understand and recall about the topics covered in the summary? (Manz 2002)

During Reading:
Use metacognitive notes to actively read your article.

Exploring Metacognition (Thinking about My Thinking)
Double-Entry Reader Response Journal for Informational Text (Template)

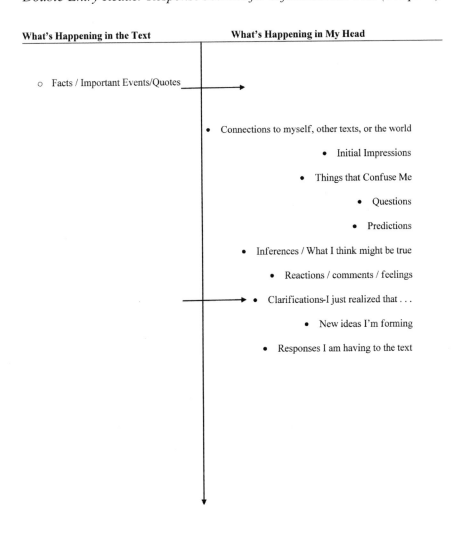

What's Happening in the Text   **What's Happening in My Head**

o   Facts / Important Events/Quotes

- Connections to myself, other texts, or the world
  - Initial Impressions
  - Things that Confuse Me
  - Questions
  - Predictions
- Inferences / What I think might be true
  - Reactions / comments / feelings
- Clarifications–I just realized that . . .
  - New ideas I'm forming
- Responses I am having to the text

Appendix B

Name: _____   Date: _____

Exploring Metacognition (Thinking about My Thinking)
Double-Entry Reader Response Journal for Informational Text

What's Happening in the Text	What's Happening in My Head

After Reading: Speed Dating through Metacognition
Anderson and Krathwohl (2001) helped redefine Bloom's taxonomy. The highest level of thinking is now *creating* instead of *evaluating*. *Creating* is defined as "putting elements together to form a coherent or functional whole; reorganizing elements into a new pattern or structure through generating, planning, or producing."

Directions: Creating Your "Character"

1. Revisit and reread your metacognitive notes.
2. Choose eight to ten human qualities that would best represent the main ideas of your article. Include them below and explain why you chose them for your character.

Table B.7

Quality	Why You Possess That Quality. Use Support from the Article

3. Now create a persona around those qualities. In the next class you will need to become that character. You will be speed dating through this metacognitive experience. That means you will have two minutes to try to "snag a date." Be prepared to answer the following questions from your possible future dates:
   - What do you do for fun?
   - How do you like to spend your spare time?
   - If you won the lottery, how would you spend your millions? Why?
   - What do you think is the most important value in a relationship?
   - What is one thing about yourself that you would like me to know?
   - What are you looking for in a relationship?

- If we went on a date, where would you take me? Why did you choose that?
- What do you believe is really important about raising children?
- What would you consider your best qualities?
- What are you most proud of?
- What is your most treasured possession and why?
- What is one job in the world that you would love to do? Explain your answer.
- What makes you laugh? Cry? Get angry?
- If you could travel back through time, what single mistake would you correct in your life? Explain your answer.
- What three adjectives would a close friend use to describe you? Explain your answer.

Speed Dating through Metacognition

Directions: Choosing your date

Before you begin to speed date, you will need to answer the questions on the previous page according to how your author or the new character you have developed would answer them. Use your reading to delve into the character, opinions, and values of the author and become that person or someone like him or her.

You will have two minutes to interview each potential date. Choose the top five questions that you believe would be most important to the author or character you have created. Be open minded. It could be that your perfect match may not think exactly as you do, but may complement your thinking in a positive way.

Complete a speed dating ticket during and/or after each interview.

Table B.8

Potential Date: _____				
From the interview, how compatible are we?				
Nothing in common		Some things in common		A perfect match
1	2	3	4	5

Something he or she said that really impressed me:

What opinions and values do you share?

What potential "red flags" do you foresee in a possible relationship? Explain your answer comparing the important ideas from the articles.

Speed Dating through Metacognition

Directions: The Debrief—Your Perfect Date!!
Reread and reflect on your speed dates. Who do you believe would be the best date for you? Why is he or she the best match for you? Support this answer with information from your reading. Be creative. Think beyond the surface and dig deep.

_____

_____

_____

_____

_____

_____

Debriefing Metacognition
In Bloom's Taxonomy revised, *creating* and *synthesizing* are the highest level of thought (combining elements into a pattern not clearly there before). Some of the verbs used when working at this level are choose, create, develop, make up, role-play, and originate. Do you believe you achieved the highest level of thinking through this activity? Explain your answer.

_____

_____

_____

_____

_____

_____

The Water Cycle—Igniting Your Thinking

Name: _____

Directions: 53-second Free Write
Answer the following essential questions to the best of your ability. Try to get whatever comes to mind down on paper. Don't worry about being right or wrong, just keep writing. You just might make some connections and remember things you learned in the last lesson or in some lesson in the past.

Essential Questions:

1. FIRST TRY:

How does the water cycle exist as a continuous flow around us? Why do you think this is important for us to know?

2. REVISIT, RETHINK, & REVISE: Reread your original answer. Is there something you would like to revise or add to it? Go ahead and revise and add to your thinking below.

How does the water cycle exist as a continuous flow around us? Why do you think this is important for us to know?

3. FINAL REVISIT, RETHINK, & REVISE: Reread your original answer. Is there something you would like to revise or add to it? Go ahead and revise and add to your thinking below.

How does the water cycle exist as a continuous flow around us? Why do you think this is important for us to know?

Appendix C

Resources for Chapter 4:
"Lifelong Learners Are Divergent Thinkers"

In *An Anchor Lesson on Visualization Using Picture Books,* by Ann Moorcones, Ann recommends using *Where the River Begins* by Thomas Locker in the following anchor lesson. Other picture books that are also valuable for teaching visualizing are listed in chapter 4.

1. *Explain the strategy*: Today we're going to be talking about a strategy that we use as good readers while we are reading. It helps us comprehend what we are reading. I'm wondering how many of you find yourself seeing what is happening in the story in a picture in your mind—like creating a movie in your head. I do. When I'm reading I am constantly using what the author is telling me and what I already know to create pictures in my mind. I picture what the characters or the setting looks like in the story, and I sometimes even see the action—just like a movie in my mind. When we create these pictures or movies in our minds while we read we are *visualizing* the story.
   - Take a minute to think about a time you visualized while reading.
   - Now pair up with a partner and talk about the pictures you created in your mind.
   - Have a few students share out their visualizations.
2. *Explain the purpose*: When we visualize while reading we are using our past experiences and the words and ideas in the story to create pictures/movies in our minds. Visualizing helps us understand the text better and makes reading more enjoyable.

3. *Share your thinking through modeling*: Today we are going to be practicing visualizing as we read the book *Where the River Begins* by Thomas Locker. (Have the front cover hidden so students are not given any clues as to Locker's interpretation of his words.) I am going to read a part of our story and share my visualizing with you as I think aloud. Your job is to listen as I read and share my thinking so we can talk about what you hear me visualizing. (Do not show the pictures.)

- Read: "Once there were two boys named Josh and Aaron who lived with their family in a big yellow house. Nearby was a river that flowed gently into the sea. On summer evenings the boys liked to sit on their porch watching the river and making up stories about it. Where, they wondered, did the river begin?"
- Share: Oh, this reminds me of visits I've made to my friend's lake house, so I can visualize the big yellow house with the river right beside it. I can also hear birds chirping and the flowing of the water. This helps me understand how peaceful it is there and how much fun the boys would have there, telling stories and wondering where the water in the river came from.
- Read: "Their grandfather loved the river and had lived near it all his life. Perhaps he would know. One day Josh and Aaron asked their grandfather to take them on a camping trip to find the beginning of the river. When he agreed, they made plans and began to pack."
- Model: I can visualize the excitement in Josh and Aaron's faces when Grandfather agreed to take them to where the river begins. I bet they jump up and down and cheer just like I do when I find out that I'm going on vacation or even out for ice cream. I know when I go camping that I always take a sleeping bag and a backpack full of food and utensils, so I see those as some of the things the boys will pack for their trip.
- Share:
  - Take a minute to think about what I visualized and how it helped me understand the story.
  - Now share this with your partner.
  - Allow a few students to share out their thinking.

4. *Practice with students*: Now it's your turn to read and share your visualizations with us. Close your eyes as I read and listen to the author's words. Think about what you see happening in the story. Be ready to share your visualizations with your partner.

   • Read: "They started out early in the next morning. For a time they walked along a familiar road past fields of golden wheat and sheep grazing in the sun. Nearby flowed the river—gentle, wide, and deep."

   • Share:
     • Think about what you visualized and what words the author used to help you with your pictures.
     • Share your visualization with your partner.
     • Allow a few students to share out their thinking.

   • Read: "At last they reached the foothills of the mountains. The road had ended and now the river would be their only guide. It raced over rocks and boulders and had become so narrow that the boys and their grandfather could jump across it."

   • Share:
     • Think about what you visualized and what words the author used to help you with your pictures.
     • Share your visualization with your partner.
     • Allow a few students to share out their thinking.

5. *Closure*: Let's think about how visualizing as we were reading today helped us understand the story better. I know that it helped me see the excitement in the boys' faces when they found out that Grandfather agreed to take them to where the river begins.

   • How did visualizing help you better understand the story?

6. Many teachers have a difficult time not finishing a story, and this book lends itself so well to visualizing a possible idea that it will allow students to read the rest of the book while they continue to practice and discuss their visualizations.

   • Make copies of the first four pages of the text you read on day one and let students illustrate one of their choice. These can be shared along with the author's pictures the next day, when the whole group meets to reread those pages. This is a great time to discuss how the experiences we bring to our reading affect our understanding. Then . . .

Make copies of the rest of the text pages in the book, and have students illustrate their visualizations for one of them. These can be shared along with the author's pictures the next day, when the whole group meets to read the rest of the book. The previous day's discussion on how the experiences we bring to our reading affect our understanding can continue.

7. Here are two follow-up ideas on using picture books to teach visualizing from an excellent reading specialist from the Coatesville Area School District, Mima Hydutsky:

   • Partner read alouds. One student reads aloud the first couple of pages of a children's book while the other partner either closes his or her eyes and imagines the pictures or sketches what he or she visualizes. Stop to share visualizations. Then partners switch roles.

   • Students create their own stories and read aloud, while other students listen and draw a scene they imagine happening in the story.

Alien Task Force Team Builder

Objective: Students will problem solve when working together and practice the process of coming to a consensus.

Materials:
- Raw eggs (one per group if teacher chooses option 1 or 2; six per group if teacher chooses option 3)
- Pennies for "spend a penny" brainstorming idea (three per person)
- Handout for each student (see below)
- Lots of paper towels for cleanup
- What to make available for students (enough for each group to have one):
- Drinking straws, five large marshmallows, masking tape, string, paper cup, toilet paper tube, ten Popsicle sticks, glue, a cloth handkerchief, one foot of plastic wrap, a broom, four pipe cleaners

Story Problem (News Flash) to Read before the Activity
First news flash if teacher chooses options 1 or 2 below:
URGENT NEWS FLASH TO EVERYONE ON EARTH
Attention, citizens of Earth! Aliens from planet Eggstra have invaded our world and attacked. Their attack is of the most unusual kind. The evil Eggstras have placed deadly egg bombs in very strategic places . . . places that will do the most damage to our world. But do not panic, the U.S. government has formed an elite task force to locate and defuse these egg bombs . . . so do not worry. Stay in your homes and close to your television for further reports. (Story provided by K. M. Walton)

Second news flash if teacher chooses option 3 below:
URGENT NEWS FLASH TO EVERYONE ON EARTH
Attention! Attention! Aliens from planet Eggtoe have invaded Earth. Their attack is of the most unusual kind. The actual feet of an Eggtoenian are lethal weapons, ready to fire liquid death at any time. But they have a terrible problem—back on planet Eggtoe their feet are misfiring. A lot. They have invaded Earth because of our ability to work together and problem solve. So, the Eggtoenians have given Earthlings an ultimatum: Help them by creating Eggtoenian shoes using what they've brought from their

planet . . . or they will invade with full force. An elite problem-solving task force has been assembled with America's deepest thinkers. Our fate rests in their hands. (Story provided by K. M. Walton)

Ways for the teacher to choose how to test the eggs:

1. Drop the egg from at least eight feet off the ground.
2. Drop the egg from eight feet up while the team lies on the ground below. (This would be crazy, but fun.)
3. Challenge students to make a pair of shoes out of six eggs (three per shoe) and have a team member walk across the room in them without cracking any of them.

Directions:

1. Read one of the stories above to set the stage. If you decide that students will do the egg drop (choices 1 or 2), read the first story. If you decide to use the egg shoes, then read the second story.
2. Display possible materials at a table and have each group look at the items and individually and quietly decide on the four items they would choose to create the egg holder (or shoes).
3. Have each person share their choices with the group.
4. Write the various choices on a 3 x 5 card and lay them face up at the center of the group.
5. Give out three pennies per person.
6. Have each student "spend their pennies" according to what they want to use to create the egg holder. They can spend all three pennies on one item if they feel strongly about it, or they can divvy up the pennies however they want to.
7. Using the "spend a penny" activity, have groups come to a consensus and choose their top four items and gather materials.
8. Using the handout, each person should quietly sketch an idea for a "two-minute quick draw."
9. Share sketches and come to a consensus.
10. Start the building. Make sure each group is secretive, as they don't want to give any ideas away.
11. Let the experiment begin!
12. Reflect using the handout.

An Alien Invasion

Name: _____

Quietly listen to the devastating news report that your teacher is going to share.

Directions to Elite Task Force:

You have been chosen for your bravery and intelligence; you are the best of the best! The country needs you . . . the entire world needs you. Your job is simple yet incredibly complex:

1. Look at the possible material choices. Which four things do you believe would be most useful?

   _____
   _____
   _____
   _____

2. Now share your ideas with your team members. Explain why you think each item is important. Write each person's choices on a 3 x 5 card (do *not* repeat choices).

3. Each team member gets three pennies. Place your pennies on the items you believe are the most important to use. If you really want to make sure one of the items is picked, you can place all three of your pennies on the card. If you want to place two pennies on one choice and one penny on a second, you can do that too, or you can place one penny on three different items. That is up to you, but once your pennies are placed on the 3 x 5 card, you cannot remove them, so place them carefully.

4. The four items with the most pennies are your team's items of choice. You may go to the materials table to collect your stuff.

5. Now, I want you to do a "two minute silent quick draw." What creation automatically comes to mind? Start drawing. Remember, this is silent and independent.

Table C.1

Two-Minute Silent Quick Draw

6. Two minutes are over. Now share your sketches with your team members. You will need to come to a consensus before building. Talk to each other, problem solve, and come to a decision about what you will make.
7. Share your ideas with the teacher before building. Do this very quietly so ideas are not stolen. It is the way of business, so if it happens, it happens. You will need to really be quiet in order to keep your great ideas a secret.
8. Work *together* using all of your chosen items. Remember, the fate of the world rests in your very capable hands. Work together, problem solve together, think together, make every decision together. There is no time for arguing or bossing team members around, *you must* work as a team or it will be . . . The. End. Of. The. World.
9. Let the experiments begin!
10. Reflect on the teambuilding process below.

How did you work together as a group to complete your finished product?

_____

_____

_____

_____

_____

What are the advantages of working in teams? What are some of the disadvantages?

_____

_____

_____

_____

_____

_____

If you had to do this again, what might you do differently? The same?

_____

_____

_____

_____

_____

Appendix D

Resources for Chapter 6:
"Lifelong Learners See Learning As Valuable"

Name: _____

Informational News Article Review—
Upper Elementary/Middle Level/Secondary

Important Information:

- Use a newspaper, journal, or the Internet to find an interesting informational article about the unit of study you are presently learning in class.
- Your article should be no more than one year old.
- Actively read the article using the BDA format handout attached to this paper.
- Attach a copy of the article to your review.
- Write a review of your article using the following format.
- Your review must be typed in 12pt font.

News Article Review Format:

1. Include information about the article in proper bibliographic format, like this:Author's last name, author's first initial. (Month of publication, year). Title of article. *Journal Title*. Pages.
   - A good resource for citing references is http://citationmachine.net.

2. *Summary of the article.* Summarize the article. Remember, summarizing means to tell about the most important parts of the article in your own words in a succinct way. To make a good summary, you must focus on the main ideas and include the following parts:
   - Write an opening sentence that includes the key information (try not to be too specific).
   - Gather key information, the important / main ideas.
   - Write a sentence describing each important idea.
   - Write down a summary sentence that sums everything up (gather up all the information and state it in a different way than in the opening sentence).
3. *Why is this article important?* In a paragraph, describe why the information in the article is important. What effect does this information have on our community? On the world? Be sure to use supporting details from the article! In other words, it is important to include information from the article to help support why you chose this particular topic.
4. *Questions/opinions about the article/chapter.* After reading the article, what questions do you still have about this topic? Is there something that wasn't explained very well in the article? Is there something else you want to know about this topic? Explain in a paragraph.

What is your opinion on what was presented in the article? Do you agree or disagree? Why or why not? Be sure to back up your opinion with facts from the article.

Scoring Guide

- Did you actively read? Did you complete and attach your BDA handout (*B*efore reading, *D*uring reading, *A*fter reading)?

1	2	3	4	5
Not Yet		OK		Wow!

- Is this a *thorough* summary of your article? Were you able to determine its importance?

1	2	3	4	5
Not Yet		OK		Wow!

- Did you support why you think the article/chapter is important, *with sufficient facts from the article*?

1	2	3	4	5
Not Yet		OK		Wow!

- Were your questions thoughtful and relative? *Was your opinion of the article/chapter supported with facts from the article*?

1	2	3	4	5
Not Yet		OK		Wow!

- *Preparation*: Is your article review on time and did you follow all format directions (including bibliography)?

1	2	3	4	5
Not Yet		OK		Wow!

Your Score: _____/25   FEEDBACK:

Active Reading: BDA Handout—Sample 1

Name: _____

<u>*Before*</u> *Reading Task*

THIEVES

Determining importance. Sometimes there is a lot of information on a page and not all of it is important. If you know where to look to find what's important, it will help you figure out how to make good predictions, and predictions keep you involved as a reader.

This prediction strategy is called THIEVES, and if you really use it, you will become smarter—guaranteed!

Before you begin, think about what thieves do. They break into a home really quickly and take whatever is important. Well, you are going to do a similar activity with reading. I want you to use the following text structures to make a prediction about what you think the most important ideas in your reading will be.

Using the THIEVES acronym, make a prediction about what you think this reading will mainly be about. Write your prediction on the next page.

T.H.I.E.V.E.S.

<u>*T . . . TITLE*</u>

What is the title?

What do I already know about this topic?

What does this topic have to do with the preceding reading or chapter?

What do I think I will be reading about?

<u>*H . . . HEADINGS/SUBHEADINGS*</u>

What does this heading tell me I will be reading about?

What is the topic of the paragraph beneath it?

How can I turn this heading into a question that is likely to be answered in the text?

<u>*I . . . INTRODUCTION*</u>

Is there an opening paragraph, perhaps italicized?

Does the first paragraph introduce the article or chapter?

What does the introduction tell me I will be reading about?

<u>*E . . . EVERY FIRST SENTENCE IN A PARAGRAPH*</u>

What do I think this article is going to be about, based on the first sentence in each paragraph?

V . . . VISUALS AND VOCABULARY

Does the article include photographs, drawings, maps, charts, or graphs?
What can I learn from the visuals in the article?
How do the captions help me better understand the meaning?
Is there a list of key vocabulary terms and definitions?
Are there important words in boldface type throughout the text?
Do I know what the boldfaced words mean?
Can I tell the meaning of the boldfaced words from the sentences in which they are embedded?

E . . . END-OF-TEXT QUESTIONS

What do the questions ask?
What information do I learn from the questions?

S . . . SUMMARY

What do I understand and recall about the topics covered in the summary?

From using the THIEVES before-reading technique, write down what you predict will be the most important ideas in the reading.

_____

_____

During Reading Task

Use sticky notes to actively read your news article. You can use any of the following sentence starters as a guide to helping you learn to actively read: "I wonder . . ." "I see . . . " "This reminds me of . . ." "I infer . . . because . . ." "I predict . . . because . . ." "I conclude . . ." (provided with permission from Stephanie Pierce).

Place your five sticky notes below.
My ideas while reading . . .

Sticky note #1—   Sticky note #2—

Sticky note #3—   Sticky note #4—

Sticky note #5—

After Reading Task

Use the space below to reflect on your learning today by writing a GIST Statement (most important ideas in a very short version). That means simply tell the gist of the article in twenty words or less. Use each line below for one word. You don't have to use all twenty lines, but you can't use more than twenty words. Your GIST statement can consist of individual words that reflect the most important ideas of the learning, or it can be in complete sentences summarizing what you learned.

GIST Statement

_____	_____	_____	_____
_____	_____	_____	_____
_____	_____	_____	_____
_____	_____	_____	_____
_____	_____	_____	_____

Active Reading: BDA Handout—Sample 2

Name: _____

Before **Reading Task**

Before reading. Use the following *scrolling and skimming* technique to predict what the reading will be about. This will help you read with a purpose in mind and will help keep you engaged—and it has been proven to make you smarter.

1. *Scrolling.* To *move the eyes quickly over an article* to determine what the information is about or if the information is relevant to what you need to find.
   - What supports are there to help you find out what it's all about?
     - Boldface words
     - Headings
     - Photographs
     - Tables, graphs, diagrams, maps
     - Illustrations
     - Examples
     - Captions
     - Sidebars

   From your scrolling, what do you predict your reading will be about? You need to write at least a two sentence prediction.
2. *Skimming.* To *read quickly* for main ideas or supporting details in a text.
   - What is the topic?
   - What challenges might you be prepared for?
   - Is this a topic which is new to you, or do you know something about it?

What questions come to mind as you begin to read? Questions are often thought of as the glue to engagement. Keep them in the forefront of your mind as you read and take note when you have answered them. It is okay if questions are not answered. They will motivate you to continue the learning.

Questions to Move You Forward in the Reading:

_____

_____

_____

_____

_____

_____

During *Reading Task*

Use sticky notes, your VIP Active Reading Card, or a pen to actively read the article. Active reading means you are not passive, but you are thinking while you read. You will know if this is happening if you are asking questions, searching for what seems important, you feel some emotion about what you are reading, you are confirming your original predictions, and you continue to predict throughout the reading. If you are tuning out, you quickly pull yourself back into the reading by rereading a bit, clarifying what you've read to check for understanding, and/or looking over how you have responded to the reading thus far.

After *Reading Task*

If you were to design a reality TV show based on your article, what would it be called, who might be members of the cast, and what would it be about? Be specific and give reasons for your choices.

_____

_____

_____

_____

_____

_____

_____

Before, During, and After Questions for Problem-Solving

Before solving:

- First, make a guesstimate by asking; what would be a reasonable answer? How do I know that is reasonable? Do my thoughts make mathematical sense?
- What visual representations can I make to help me understand the problem better?
- Have I solved a similar problem? If so, what strategies did I use to solve that problem? If not, what connections can I make to help make this problem easier to understand?
- What are my givens?
- What do I need to find out?
- What are my constraints in the problem? How do I know?
- How is today's lesson similar to yesterday's lesson? How will that help me solve the problem?
- How might I get started? Does this make sense?
- What inferences can I make about…? Explain your inference.

During solving:

- Is what I am doing so far making sense with my original estimate? Why? Why not? If not, what will I do differently and why?
- What am I doing to solve this problem and why am I doing it? Does it make sense?

After solving:

- Does my answer make sense?
- Are my strategy and answer reasonable?
- Does my answer align with my original estimate? If so, how? If not, what do I need to do differently? Why?
- How do I know I am right?
- Is there another way I could have solved this problem? How? Why did I choose the method I did?
- What questions might I still have about…? (Pearse & Walton 2011)

Connecting Arithmetic to Algebra
8-4-2 Homework Menu

Name: _____   Due Date: _____

Directions: Now that it's November, it's time to start handling homework the way the seventh and eighth graders do—with choice, determination, and great effort!

1. You need to complete 10 points worth of work for the week. How you do that is up to you. See all the possible options to choose from below.
2. Keep careful track of your work using this page and your work folder. Remember, you are in charge of managing your time. Do it wisely!!
3. Check off below every time you complete one option; place all completed work in the "In Box."
4. Every day when you get to class, look in the "Out Box" for your graded work.
5. Take it back and add the grade you received in the box below.
6. Keep all your work organized in your work folder.

8 points	8 points	8 points
Maid to Order	***Crack the Codes***	***Follow the Rules***
Include all your calculations and staple it to the completed handout. You must also do the Bonus Box and include that with your work. Be thoughtful. ◯ Check off when completed.	Include all your work and a full explanation of how you figure out the codes. Staple it to the completed handout. Be thoughtful. ◯ Check off when completed.	Include all your work and a full explanation of how you figure out the codes. You must also do the Bonus Box and include that with your work. ◯ Check off when completed.
4 points	4 points	4 points
Carnival Roundup	***Rat Race***	***The Great Disappearance***
Play the game with a partner. Complete a "Proof of Game form" ◯ Check off when completed.	Play the game with a partner. Complete a "Proof of Game form" ◯ Check off when completed.	All the numbers have disappeared. Use your math sense to decide on the appropriate operation. Then, ***explain how you know*** ◯ Check off when completed.
2 points	2 points	2 points
Peg's Patchwork Quilt	***Unlucky Ladybug***	***Place Value Puzzle***
Be neat, be accurate. ◯ Check off when completed.	Be neat, be accurate. ◯ Check off when completed.	Be neat, be accurate. ◯ Check off when completed.

Name:_____

Directions: Choose your own assignment! You must complete three activities in a tic-tac-toe design. Each row is designed according to Webb's Depth of Knowledge. Choose any three ideas that create a tic-tac-toe design. You may go vertically, horizontally, or diagonally.

Naturalist	Musical	Verbal Linguistic
While at home, go outside and collect 6 different rocks. Draw a picture of each rock in your journal. Then bring your rocks to school and identify the type of each rock telling what clues let you to know if it was sedimentary, metamorphic, or igneous. Be prepared to teach what you learned to small groups during menu time.	Create a "Rock" song or rap. It must have a main theme in both melody and lyrics. The lyrics should convey accurate scientific information and should be creative and the details should support the main theme. A live performance is required and must be rehearsed well in advance. You can write a song using a familiar tune to tell how a type of rock (sedimentary, igneous, and metamorphic) is formed.	Using art materials, the directions for creating a game board, and all of your gained knowledge from research, create a board game that test players' knowledge of Rocks. You must first research and include 20 facts from research. (See Checkpoint Packet – 5 points). You may do this alone or with a partner.
Visual Spatial/Computer	**Computer**	**Visual Spatial/Interpersonal**
Using the following site for research http://library.thinkquest.org/J002289/index.html Design one Venn Diagram comparing two rocks and one tree map that identifies the properties of a rock. Give examples of each property (luster, color, streak, hardness, etc.).	Complete the "Name That Rock" Game. Record your score on the score sheet. http://library.thinkquest.org/J002289/name.html Complete the "Famous Rock Scavenger Hunt" Game. http://library.thinkquest.org/J002289/index.html	Along with a partner, create a class bulletin board. The science presented must be accurate, interesting and clear. The display needs to be a work of art with a strong factual background. It needs to catch and hold the attention of the audience, and it must be clearly seen several from all points in the room.
Interpersonal	**Body Kinesthetic**	**Intrapersonal**
Create 10 Rock Trading Cards *Include a definition and a picture for each rock.* Your trading cards should resemble a real set, These will also be used as a resource in the class, so it needs to be your very best work. It should be neat, scientifically accurate, creative, and show a lot of effort.	Use clay to create a model of each type of rock (sedimentary, igneous, and metamorphic). Label each type of rock. Include information you learned about each type of rock in your demonstration. Your classmates will prepare questions for you to answer in your research.	Complete 10 journal entries using the high level question cards that your teacher will provide. Each entry should be at least ½ page. It needs to be well thought and neatly written. Design a cover for your journal that would show your understanding of rocks.

Appendix E

Resources for Chapter 7:
"Lifelong Learners Are Collaborative"

Clock Partners

(created by Christina MacRae for Margie Pearse & Kate Walton, 2011)

The Jigsaw

DIRECTIONS FOR STUDENTS

1. Begin with your HOME group. Number off 1–4. Each person will be leaving their home group to form expert groups according to your number. (For example, all #1s will go to a designated area, etc.)

2. You will also notice that the reading is labeled and broken into four sections. Which number are you? Your number tells you what section you are to read in the text. Locate the section of the text you are responsible for.

3. Actively read your section in the text, silently and thoroughly. Use the accompanying B-D-A handout to guide you on your Active Reading journey. (See appendix E for a sample BDA reading task.)

4. Go to EXPERT Group.—With your expert group, share your three most important points and compare notes.
   - Discuss as a group.
   - Come to an "expert group agreement" on what three points you will all share when you get back to your Home Groups.

5. Return to your HOME Group with your new knowledge from the reading.
   - Each expert will take a turn teaching the three most important points and any other critical information from their section.
   - The other home group members should listen and learn enough from each expert presentation to complete the final home group task.
   - In other words, pay attention to each group member's presentation—it is your responsibility.

6. With your HOME Group, the final task is to produce a creative representation of what your reading means to you.
   - Use poster paper and markers.
   - You must include important information from each section.
   - Your poster will be on display for the whole class to see. Please give it your all—work together—be creative—be thorough—show that you care.

The Jigsaw Classroom
"Out for Blood" (*Yes! Mag* 2010, no. 17)

Begin with your home group (2 people per group). Number off 1–2. Each person will be leaving his or her home group to form expert partnerships according to number. (For example, if you are a #1, find another #1 to form an expert group.)

Go to expert groups. With your expert group (that is, you and a partner), you will be responsible for first previewing the text by scrolling and skimming, *silently reading* your assigned part of the text, and following the directions for each assignment.

Return to your home group with all your new knowledge from the reading.

1. Each expert should take turns sharing a little about the *most important ideas* from the reading.
2. The other home group partner should be listening and learning.
3. Take turns reporting all you learned from your expert group to each home group member.

Complete one of the following options with your home group:

- Create a *poster illustrating a cover for a science magazine.* Include the most important ideas and visuals from the article you read. Make it appealing! Draw the reader in. Be creative. Make sure everyone's reading piece is represented in the cover.
- Come to a consensus. Which "blood sucker" would you say is the most dangerous to humans? Create a Wanted Poster for what you consider to be the most dangerous blood sucker. Be creative!! Use all your knowledge to make your poster believable. You can go back to the reading for facts. You must include the following in your Wanted Poster:

Important "facts" to include that make this creature the most dangerous:

1. "Mug shot" (an illustration)
2. An aka (also known as . . .)
3. What is it wanted for?
4. Its last known location

Halloween Jigsaw—BDA Active Reading
"Out for Blood" (*Yes! Mag* 2010, no. 17, pp. 15–16)

EXPERT #1   Name: _____

Expert #1—Reading assignment: pages 15 and 16 (you are working in partnership with another Expert #1)

<u>*Before*</u> *Reading Strategy*

Scrolling the text features and *skimming* to predict (silently and independently)

Scrolling: To move the eyes quickly over an article to determine what the information is about or if the information is relevant to what you need to find.

What supports are there to help you find out what it's all about?

1. Boldface words
2. Headings
3. Photographs
4. Illustrations
5. Captions
6. Sidebars

Skimming: To read quickly for main ideas or supporting details in a text.

What is the topic? _____

Why do you think this is important to learn? _____

What question(s) come to mind from the skimming? _____

Sharing: Share your predictions and questions with your expert partner.

<u>*During*</u> *Reading Strategy*</u>

Read silently. Ask yourself, "What information do I feel is the most important part of what I am reading under each heading?" Use sticky notes marked VIP (Very Important Part) to highlight what you determine to be most important.

After **Reading Strategy**

- Discuss with your expert partner the most important ideas you came up with. Listen and learn.
- Answer the following question: *Why do you think this information is important?*
- Go back to your home group to share all you've learned. You will be using this knowledge to create something together.

Halloween Jigsaw—BDA Active Reading
"Out for Blood" (*Yes! Mag* 2010, no. 17, pp. 17–18)

EXPERT #2   Name: _____

Expert #2—Reading Assignment: pages 17 and 18 (you are working in partnership with another Expert #2)

<u>*Before* Reading Strategy</u>

Scrolling the text features and *skimming* to predict (silently and independently)

Scrolling: To move the eyes quickly over an article to determine what the information is about or if the information is relevant to what you need to find.

What supports are there to help you find out what it's all about?

1. Boldface words
2. Headings
3. Photographs
4. Illustrations
5. Captions
6. Sidebars

Skimming: To read quickly for main ideas or supporting details in a text.

What is the topic? _____

Whydoyouthinkthisisimportanttolearn?_____

Whatquestion(s)cometomindfromtheskimming?_____

Sharing: Share your predictions and questions with your expert partner.

<u>*During* Reading Strategy</u>

Read silently. Ask yourself, "What information do I feel is the most important part of what I am reading under each heading?" Use sticky notes marked VIP (Very Important Part) to highlight what you determine to be most important.

<u>*After* Reading Strategy</u>

- Discuss with your expert partner the most important ideas you came up with. Listen and learn.

- Answer the following question: *Why do you think this information is important?*
- Go back to your home group to share all you've learned. You will be using this knowledge to create something together.

References

Allen, J. (1999). *Words, words, words: Teaching vocabulary in grades 4–12.* Portland, ME: Stenhouse.

Allen, J. (2000). *Yellow brick roads: Shared and guided paths to independent reading 4–12.* Portland, ME: Stenhouse.

Allington, R. L. (2006). *What really matters for struggling readers: Designing research-based programs* (2nd ed.). Upper Saddle River, NJ: Pearson Education.

Anderson, L. W., & Krathwohl, D. R. (Eds.). (2001). *A taxonomy for learning, teaching and assessing: A revision of Bloom's Taxonomy of educational objectives.* New York: Longman

Andrew, S., & Vialle, W. (1998). Nursing students' self-efficacy, self-regulated learning, and academic performance in science. http://www.aare.edu.au/98pap/and98319.htm

Bandura, A. (1992). Exercise of personal agency through the self-efficacy mechanisms. In R. Schwarzer (Ed.), *Self-efficacy: Thought control of action.* Washington, DC: Hemisphere.

Bandura, A. (1994). Self-efficacy. In V. S. Ramachaudran (Ed.), *Encyclopedia of human behavior* (Vol. 4, pp. 71–81). New York: Academic Press.

Bandura, A. (1995). *Self-efficacy in changing societies.* Cambridge, England: Cambridge University Press.

Beers, K. (2003). *When kids can't read: What teachers can do.* Portsmouth, NH: Heinemann.

Bell, B., & Cowie, B. (2000). *Formative assessment and science education.* Portsmouth, NH: Heinemann.

Beninghof, A. (2006). *Engage all students through differentiation.* Peterborough, NH: Crystal Springs Books.

Beninghof, A. (2010). *Turning best practice into daily practice: Simple strategies for the busy teacher.* Peterborough, NH: Crystal Springs Books.

Bernard, B. (2005). *Resiliency: What we have learned.* San Francisco: West Ed.

Bloom, B. S. (1985). *Developing talent in young people.* New York: Ballantine Books.

Burke, Jim. (1998). 103 things to do before/during/after reading. *English Teacher's Companion.* Portsmouth, NH: Boyntono-Cook. Accessed 9 April 2013, from http://englishcompanion.com/assignments/reading/103readingactivities.htm

Charney, R. (2002). *Teaching children to care: Classroom management for ethical and academic growth K-8.* Greenfield, MA: Northeast Foundation for Children.

Cohen, J. (1999). *Educating minds and hearts: Social emotional learning and the passage into adolescence.* New York, NY: Teachers College Press.

Cohen, L., & Spenciner, L. (2010). *Assessment of children and youth with special needs* (4th ed.). Upper Saddle River, NJ: Pearson.

Costa, A. (2008). The thought-filled curriculum. *Educational Leadership, 65*(5), 20–24.

Costa, A., & Kallick, B. (2000). *Assessing and reporting habits of mind.* Alexandria, VA: Association for Supervision and Curriculum Development (ASCD).

Costa, A., & Kallick, B. (2009). *Habits of mind across the curriculum: Practical and creative strategies for teachers.* Alexandria, VA: Association for Supervision and Curriculum Development (ASCD).

Covey, S. R. (2004). *The 7 Habits of Highly Effective People.* New York: Free Press.

Crawley, J. (2005). *In at the deep end: A survival guide for teachers in post compulsory education.* London: David Fulton.

Csikszentmihalyi, Mihaly. (1990). *The psychology of optimal experience.* New York: Harper-Collins Publishing.

Csikszentmihalyi, M. (1997). *Finding flow: The psychology of engagement with everyday life.* New York: Basic Books.

Csikszentmihalyi, M., Abuhamdeh, S., & Nakamura, J. (2005). Flow. In A. Elliot & C. Dweck (Eds.), *Handbook of competence and motivation* (pp. 598–608). New York: Guilford Press.

Daniels, H., & Steineke, N. (2011). *Text and lessons for content-area reading.* Portsmouth, NH: Heinemann.

Deci, E. (2006, August 30). Student motivation: what works, what doesn't. Transcript, Edweek.org online chat, at http://www.edweek.org/chat/transcript_08_30_06.html

Denton, P., & Kriete, R. (2000). *The first six weeks of school.* Greenfield, MA: Northeast Foundation for Children.

Dewey, J. (1933). *How we think: A restatement of the relation of reflective thinking to the educative process.* Boston: Heath.

Dweck, C. S. (2006). *Mindset: The new psychology of success.* New York: Ballantine Books.

Elbow, P. (1998a). *Writing with power: Techniques for mastering the writing process* (2nd ed.). New York: Oxford University Press.

Elbow, P. (1998b). *Writing without teachers.* New York: Oxford University Press.

Erwin, J. C. (2010). *Inspiring the best in students.* Alexandria, VA: Association for Supervision and Curriculum Development (ASCD).

Fisher, D., & Frey, N. (2007). *Checking for understanding: Formative assessment techniques for your classroom.* Alexandria, VA: Association for Supervision and Curriculum Development (ASCD).

Focus on effectiveness. (n.d.). NETC.org. Accessed 9 April 2013, at http://www.netc.org/focus/strategies/sett.php

Forget, M. A. (2004). *Max teaching with reading and writing: Classroom activities for helping students learn new subject matter while acquiring literacy skills.* Victoria, BC, Canada: Trafford.

Forsten, C., Grant, J., & Hollas, B. (2002). *Differentiated instruction: Different strategies for different learners.* Peterborough, NH: Crystal Springs Books.

Fountas, I., & Pinnell, G. (2001). *Guiding readers and writers.* Portsmouth, NH: Heinemann.

Fuhrken, C. (2009). *What every elementary teacher needs to know about reading tests (from someone who has written them).* Portland, ME: Stenhouse.

Garofalo, R., Jr. (2008). *A winner by any standard: 52 character challenges for teens.* Hartford, CT: Teen Winners Publishing.

Gay, G. (2000). *Culturally responsive teaching: Theory, research, and practice.* New York: Teachers College Press.

Get motivated. (n.d.). President's challenge. Accessed 9 April, 2013, at http://www.presidentschallenge.org/motivated/setting-goals.shtml

Gibbs, J. (2006). *Reaching all by creating tribes learning communities.* Windsor, CA: CenterSource Systems.

Glasser, W. (1998). *Choice theory: A new psychology of personal freedom.* New York: HarperCollins.

Goleman, D. (1995). *Emotional intelligence: Why it can matter more than IQ.* New York: Bantam.

Gregory, G., & Chapman, C. (2002). *Differentiated instruction: One size doesn't fit all.* Thousand Oaks, CA: Corwin Press.

Gregory, G. H., & Parry, T. (2006). *Designing brain-compatible learning* (3rd ed.). Thousand Oaks, CA: Corwin Press.

Harvey, S., & Goudvis, A. (2007). *Strategies that work: Teaching comprehension for understanding and engagement.* Portland, ME: Stenhouse.

Harwayne, S. (1992). *Lasting impressions.* Portsmouth, NH: Heinemann.

Hattie, J., Biggs, J., & Purdie, N. 1996. Effects of learning skills interventions on student learning. A meta-analysis. *Review of Education Research, 66*(2), 99–136.

Haworth, M. (2011, March 28). Top 10 strategic thinking skills. Improvement and Innovation. http://www.improvementandinnovation.com/features/article/top10-strategic thinkingskills/

Heath, C. & Heath, D. (2010). *Switch: How to change things when change is hard.* New York: Crown Publishing.

Hollas, B. (2005). *Differentiating instruction in a whole-group setting (Grades 3–8).* Peterborough, NH: Crystal Springs Books.

Horn, S. (2012, September 21). 5 tips to improve your concentration, at http://altmedicine.about.com/od/optimumhealthessentials/a/Concentration.htm

Hyatt, C., & Gottlieb, L. (1993). *Benjamin Barber: an eminent sociologist.* New York: Penguin Books.

Hyde, A. (2006). *Comprehending math: Adapting reading strategies to teach mathematics, K–6.* Portsmouth, NH: Heinemann.

Hyde, A. (2009). *Understanding middle school math.* Portsmouth, NH: Heinemann.

Jackson, R. (2009). *Never work harder than your students, and other principles of great teaching.* Alexandria, VA: Association for Supervision and Curriculum Development (ASCD).

Jackson, R. (2011a). *How to motivate reluctant learners* (Mastering the principles of great teaching). Alexandria, VA: Association for Supervision and Curriculum Development (ASCD).

Jackson, R. (2011b). *How to plan rigorous instruction* (Mastering the principles of great teaching). Alexandria, VA: Association for Supervision and Curriculum Development (ASCD).

Jensen, E. (1997). *Completing the puzzle: The brain-compatible approach to learning* (2nd ed.). Del Mar, CA: Turning Point.

Jensen, E. (1998). *Introduction to brain-compatible learning.* Del Mar, CA: Turning Point.

Jensen, E. (2006). *Enriching the brain: How to maximize every learner's potential.* San Francisco: Jossey-Bass.

Johnson, D. W., & Johnson, R. T. (1999). *Learning together and alone: Cooperative, competitive, and individualistic learning* (5th ed.). Needham Heights, ME: Allyn & Bacon.

Johnson, D. W., Johnson, R. T., & Roseth, C. (2006). Do peer relationships affect achievement? *The Cooperative Link, 21*(1), 2–4.

Jones, R. (n.d.). ReadingQuest: Making sense in social studies. http://www.readingquest.org

Jones, S. (2003). *Blueprint for student success: A guide to research-based teaching practices.* Thousand Oaks, CA: Corwin Press.

Kagan, S., & Kagan, M. (2000). *Kagan cooperative learning: Course workbook.* San Clemente, CA: Author, at http://www.KaganOnline.com

Kagan, S., & Kagan, M. (2009). *Kagan cooperative learning.* San Clemente, CA: Author, at http:// www.KaganOnline.com

Kay, A. (2010). *Fry the monkeys create a solution: The manager's and facilitator's guide to accelerating change using solution.* Toronto, Ontario: Glasgow Group.

Keene, E. (2008). *To understand: New horizons in reading comprehension.* Portsmouth, NH: Heinemann.

Kelly, M. J., & Clausen-Grace, N. 2007. *Laying the foundation for the metacognitive teaching framework: Comprehension shouldn't be silent.* Newark, DE: International Reading Association.

Kohn, A. (1993, September). Choices for children: why and how to let students decide. *Phi Delta Kappan Magazine, 75,* 8–19.

Lehrer, J. (2009, May 18). DON'T! The secret of self-control. *New Yorker,* at http://www.newyorker.com/reporting/2009/05/18/090518fa_fact_lehrer?currentPage=1

Levels of questioning Bloom's taxonomy. TeacherVision. Accessed 8 April 2013, at http://www.teachervision.fen.com/teaching-methods/new teacher/48446.html#ixzz1dmkQsrMx

Lillie, B. (2011, August 19). Five mindshifting talks on happiness. *Ted* (blog), at http://blog.ted.com/2011/08/19/playlist-5-mindshifting-talks-on-happiness/

Maciejewski, P. J., Prigerson, H. G., & Mazure, C. M. (2000). Self-efficacy as a mediator between stressful life events and depressive symptoms. *British Journal of Psychology, 176,* 373–78.

Manz, S. L. (2002). A strategy for previewing textbooks: Teaching readers to become THIEVES. *The Reading Teacher, 55,* 434–35.

The marshmallow test. (2009, September 24). Igniter Media, at http://www.youtube.com/watch?v=QX_oy9614HQ

Marzano, R. J. (1998). *A theory-based meta-analysis of research on instruction.* Aurora, CO: Mid-Continent Regional Educational Laboratory.

Marzano, R. J. (2001). *Designing a new taxonomy of educational objectives.* Alexandria, VA: Association for Supervision and Curriculum Development (ASCD).

Marzano, R. J. (2003). *What works in schools: Translating research into action.* Alexandria, VA: Association for Supervision and Curriculum Development (ASCD).

Marzano, R. J. (2007). *The art and science of teaching: A comprehensive framework for effective instruction.* Alexandria, VA: Association for Supervision and Curriculum Development (ASCD).

Marzano, R. J., & Kendall, J. S. (2008). *Designing and assessing educational objectives: Applying the new taxonomy.* Thousand Oaks, CA: Corwin Press.

Marzano, R. J., Pickering, D. J., & Pollock, J. E. (2001). *Classroom instruction that works.* Alexandria, VA: Association for Supervision and Curriculum Development (ASCD).

Maxwell, J. C. (2009). *How successful people think.* New York: Center Street.

McKeown, D. (2011, May 5). Ken Robinson paper clip, at http://www.youtube.com/watch?v=hzBa-frc2JA

McTighe, J., & Wiggins, G. (2004). *Understanding by design: Professional development workbook.* Alexandria, VA: Association for Supervision and Curriculum Development (ASCD).

Miller, D. (2002). *Reading with meaning.* Portland, ME: Stenhouse.

Munroe, D. W., & Stevenson, J. (2009, Winter). The effects of response cards on student and teacher behavior during vocabulary instruction. *Journal of Applied Behavioral Analysis 42*(4), 795–800, http://seab.envmed.rochester.edu/jaba/articles/2009/jaba-42-04-0795.pdf

National Council of Teachers of Mathematics. (2011, January). *Journal for Research in Mathematics Education.*

National Institute of Mental Health. (2011). *Teenage brain: A work in progress. A brief overview of research into brain development during adolescence.* Bethesda, MD: Author.

Osborn, A. (1953). *Applied imagination: Principles and procedures of creative problem solving.* New York: Scribner.

Pace Marshall, S. (2003). *A new story for learning.* Paper presented at a Learning to Learn conference, Adelaide, South Australia.

Pavio, A. (1990). *Mental representations: A dual coding approach.* New York: Oxford University Press.

Pawson, E., Fournier, E., Haight, M., Muniz, O., Trafford, J., & Vajoczki, S. (2006). Problem-based learning in geography: Towards a critical assessment of its purposes, benefits and risks. *Journal of Geography in Higher Education 30*(1), 103–16.

Pearse, M., & Walton, K. M. (2011). *Teaching numeracy: Nine critical habits to ignite mathematical thinking.* Thousand Oaks, CA: Corwin Press.

Pericone, J. (2005). *Zen and the art of public school teaching*. Frederick, MD: PublishAmerica.

Pink, D. (2005). *A whole new mind: Moving from the Information Age to the Conceptual Age*. New York: Penguin Books.

Pink, D. (2009). *Drive: The surprising truth about what motivates us*. New York: Riverhead Books.

Posamentier, A. S., & Jaye, D. (2006). *What successful math teachers do, Grades 6–12*. Thousand Oaks, CA: Corwin Press.

Predicting. (n.d.). TeacherVision. Accessed 8 April 2013, at http://www.teacher -vision.fen.com/skill-builder/reading/48711.html

Quate, S., & McDermott, J. (2009). *Clockwatchers: Six steps to motivating and engaging disengaged students across content areas*. Portsmouth, NH: Heine-mann.

Ronis, D. L. (2006). *Brain-compatible mathematics* (2nd ed.). Thousand Oaks, CA: Corwin Press.

Ross, B. H. (1987). This is like that: The use of earlier problems and the separation of similarity effects. *Journal of Experimental Psychology, 13*(4), 405–37.

Scott, J., & Flanigan, E. (1996). *Achieving consensus: Tools and techniques.* Lanham, MD: National Book Network.

Sitomer, A. (2008). *Teaching teens and reaping results in a wi-fi, hip-hop, where-has-all-the-sanity-gone world*. New York: Scholastic.

Sladkey, D. (n.d.). What are energizing brain breaks? Energizing Brain Breaks. Accessed 9 April 2013, at http://www.energizingbrainbreaks.com/

Snodgrass, M. E. (2008). *Beating the odds: A teen guide to 75 superstars who overcame adv*ersity. Westport, CT: Greenwood Press.

Sousa, D. A. (2006). *How the brain learns* (3rd ed.). Thousand Oaks, CA: Corwin Press.

Sprenger, M. (2005). *How to teach so students remember*. Alexandria, VA: As-sociation for Supervision and Curriculum Development (ASCD).

Stahl, S. A., & Fairbanks, M. M. (1986). The effects of vocabulary instruction: A model-based meta-analysis. *Review of Educational Research, 56*(7), 72–110.

Sylwester, R. (2000). *A biological brain in a cultural classroom: Applying bio-logical research to the classroom management*. Thousand Oaks, CA: Corwin Press.

Tate, M. (2010). *Worksheets don't grow dendrites: 20 instructional strategies that engage the brain.* Thousand Oaks, CA: Corwin Press.

Tileston, D. W. (2010a). *What every teacher should know about student motiva-tion* (2nd ed.). Thousand Oaks, CA: Corwin Press.

Tileston, D. W. (2010b). *Training manual for* What every teacher should know. Thousand Oaks, CA: Corwin Press.

Tinzmann, M. B., et al. (1990). The collaborative classroom: Reconnecting teachers and learners. Video Conference 3, *Restructuring to Promote Learning in America's Schools, a Guidebook.* Alexandria, VA, and NCREL, Elmhurst, IL: PBS Video.

Tomlinson, C. (1999). *The differentiated classroom: Responding to the needs of all students.* Alexandria, VA: Association for Supervision and Curriculum Development (ASCD).

Tovanni, C. (2004). *Do I really have to teach reading? Content comprehension—grades 6–12.* Portland, ME: Stenhouse.

Umbach, R. Listening with understanding and empathy. *Habits of Mind.* Accessed April 9, 2013 at http://www.habitsofmind.org/

Vaca, J., Vaca, R., & Gove, M. (1987). *Reading and learning to read.* Boston: Little Brown.

Van Gelder, Sarah. (2010, October). Seeds of resilience. *Yes Magazine,* 55, 15–18.

Watson, Sam. (n.d.). *How to brainstorm in the classroom,* Special Ed. About. Accessed 8 April, 2013, at http://specialed.about.com/od/teacherstrategies/a/brainstorm.htm

Wiggins, G., & McTighe, J. (2005). *Understanding by design.* (Expanded 2nd ed.). Alexandria, VA: Association for Supervision and Curriculum Development (ASCD).

Wilhelm, J. (2002). *Action strategies for deepening comprehension: Role plays, text-structure tableaux, talking statues, and other enactment techniques that engage students with text.* New York: Scholastic.

Willis, J. (2009). *Inspiring middle school minds: Gifted, creative, and challenging.* Scottsdale, AZ: Great Potential Press.

Wormeli, R. (2009). *Metaphors and analogies: Power tools for teaching any subject.* Portland, ME: Stenhouse.

Zimmerman, S., & Hutchins, C. (2003). *Seven keys to comprehension: How to get help your kids read it and get it!* New York: Three Rivers Press.

Zinsser, W. (1988). *Writing to learn.* New York: Harper & Row.

Zwiers, J. (2004). *Building reading comprehension habits in grades 6–12.* Newark, DE: International Reading Association.

Index

About the Authors

Margie Pearse has spent over twenty-five years as an educator, instructional coach, and researcher. She has her master's degree in multicultural education with certifications in elementary education, mathematics, and English as a second language.

She is currently a math specialist and college professor at both the undergraduate and graduate levels and conducts innovative professional development on how to craft instructional practices that transform student thinking, build lifelong learners, and represent best practice. She is lead author of *Teaching Numeracy: 9 Critical Habits to Ignite Mathematical Thinking* (2011).

Her newest research focuses on empowering all students with the qualities it takes to become lifelong learners. It is groundbreaking research that is bound to make a positive impact on teaching and learning.

Her educational philosophy can be summed up as, "Why *not* reinvent the wheel? Yesterday's lessons will not suffice for students to succeed in tomorrow's world. We need to meet students not just where they are, but where they need to be. There is great potential in every child. It is our job to empower students to discover that potential and to possess the tenacity and self-efficacy to reach it."

Her passion for teaching and learning drove her to coauthor this book.

Mary Dunwoody spent more than thirty-five years in education. Her experience spans the scope from classroom teacher to principal to director of secondary teaching and learning. She holds a master's degree in education, in addition to undergraduate degrees in music and math education.

During her tenure, she developed professional learning communities with colleagues and facilitated professional development sessions across grade levels and content areas.

Retired from her full-time administrative position, she presently works as an independent educational consultant, mentoring teachers and developing effective techniques that optimize their professional practice.

Her contributions to this book provided a welcome opportunity to share a professional lifetime of experiences with learners of all ages. A lifelong learner, she continues to explore the possibilities of touching the minds and tapping the potential in every student.

Belief in the core desire within each of us to continue to grow and blossom, her goal for this book is to provide essential tools for the tool bag that educators pack daily as they prepare to meet their students.